INFO
BANK

This material was first published in 2002 by Miles Kelly Publishing Ltd
Bardfield Centre, Great Bardfield, Essex, CM7 4SL

This edition published in 2006 by Bardfield Press
Bardfield Press is an imprint of Miles Kelly Publishing Ltd
Bardfield Centre, Great Bardfield, Essex, CM7 4SL

2 4 6 8 10 9 7 5 3 1

Editorial Director: Belinda Gallagher
Art Director: Jo Brewer
Editor: Amanda Askew
Editorial Assistant: Bethanie Bourne
Designers: Candice Bekir, Stephan Davis, Venita Kidwai, Gemma Simmons
Picture Researcher: Liberty Newton
Reprographics: Anthony Cambray, Mike Coupe, Ian Paulyn

British Library Cataloguing-in-Publication Data
A catalogue record for this book is available from the British Library

ISBN 1-84236-785-4

Printed in China

www.mileskelly.net
info@mileskelly.net

Acknowledgements
Page 269 NASA
All other photographs from Miles Kelly Archives.

INFO BANK

BARDFIELD
PRESS

CONTENTS

SCIENCE 8-95

ANIMALS 96–183

CONTENTS

OUR PLANET 272-359

SCIENCE

From materials and states of matter to energy and motion, this section is bursting with amazing facts about the world of science.

How is electricity made?
What is inside an atom?
Who invented the light bulb?

Read on to find the answers to these and many other fascinating questions.

SCIENCE EXPLAINED

MATERIALS

Plastics are light, durable and colourful, but a plastic bowl melts easily over flames. Like all materials, plastics have limits. Metals and glass withstand flames better, but glass shatters when knocked hard. Composites are materials mixed specially for particular jobs.

STATES

Iron is solid. Water is liquid. Oxygen is gas. Usually – they can all change their forms, or states. Water freezes at 0°C into solid ice. With enough heat from burning fuel, iron melts into a liquid at 1535°C. Even hotter is the fourth state of matter, plasma, where particles called ions have electric charges.

MATTER

Keep splitting a substance into pieces. How far can you get? Molecules such as DNA are collections of atoms. There are more than 115 kinds of atom, such as carbon, iron and oxygen. Each is a chemical element. Atoms are made of sub-atomic particles, chiefly electrons, protons and neutrons. Smaller still are quarks.

ELECTRICITY

One of the smallest particles is the electron. Billions of them flowing along make convenient, useful energy – electricity. We measure it accurately, alter and manipulate it in many ways, from microchips to power stations, and change or convert it to other forms of energy, such as light, heat and sound.

CHEMICAL CHANGE

Our world is composed of atoms. They make up chemicals and change in reactions. Sometimes they join, in other cases they split, often helped by extra substances called catalysts. Biochemicals – such as those in the body – do this every second, as we breathe air and slow-burn or combust it, for energy.

POWER

In everyday life 'power' usually means generated electricity, most notably when it fails, in a power cut. In science, power is using energy or doing work over time. Rockets and other engines, burning fuel, splitting the nucleus of an atom, and light or heat from the Sun, are all further meanings of the term 'power'.

MOTION

Moving in straight lines and circles, rotating or spinning, and being pushed or pulled by forces such as gravity, are all governed by basic physical laws. Scientists calculate motion very carefully, so that a funfair ride stays safe and a shuttle reaches space.

MACHINES

A machine makes tasks easier. A simple lever lifts the lid off a can. A wheel lets a weight roll. Pulleys or gears move a big load with a small force. Hydraulics use pressure in liquids to the same effect. However, the laws of mechanics do not allow something for nothing. The bigger the load, the less it moves.

ENERGY

The ability to make things happen, cause change, and do work – this is energy. It takes many forms such as sound, heat, light, motion, electricity, and radioactivity from the splitting of the centres, or nuclei, of atoms. Energy can happen in bursts or pulses, like the 'pieces' of light known as photons.

WAVES

To and fro, up and down, in and out – energy moves as waves of many kinds. We use the range, or spectrum, of electromagnetic (EM) waves every day, including radio waves, microwaves, light in all its colours, X-rays and many other kinds of radiation.

PLASTICS

Features of plastic

Most plastics are made from petroleum (crude oil). They are lightweight, waterproof, tough and hard-wearing, do not rot or decay and resist the passage of heat and electricity. They can be made in a vast variety of colours, which can be are transparent or opaque. Plastics can also be shaped or moulded into almost any form, with smooth surfaces and edges. These features make plastics ideal for cases, components and other items, especially for electrical equipment such as computers, games consoles, music systems and kitchen appliances.

Early plastics

In 1907, Belgian-American chemist, Leo Baekeland (1863–1944) studied the chemical reactions between substances such as phenol and formaldehyde. He produced a dark substance that set hard when cool and did not conduct electricity. Named Bakelite, this early plastic was soon being shaped into frames and casings for electrical items.

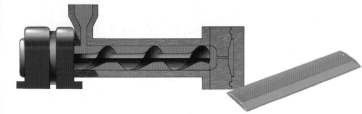

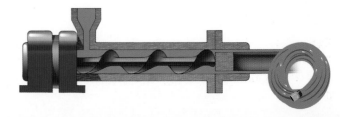

Extrusion
Plastic is heated, pressurized and then squeezed. and stretched or drawn through a narrow gap, to form a long, continuous part such as a pipe, tube or rod.

Injection
Plastic is forced or injected by a heating and screw device into a hollow shape, the mould, where it takes on the shape and then sets hard.

Practical plastic
Nearly all of the handset and console is moulded from plastics of different types and colours. They are strong, light and do not conduct electricity, forming a safe exterior.

Retro plastic
The Bakelite telephone could be found in most homes during the 1930s and 1940s and continues to be a popular choice today due to its durability and retro appeal.

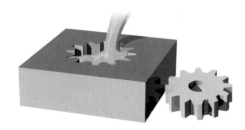

Stamping and pressing
A block of plastic is pressed hard and fast into the required shape.

Moulding
Molten, runny plastic is poured into a shaped mould. As it cools it goes solid and hard.

COMPOSITES

Purpose-made combinations

A composite is a material made from a combination of other single substances, such as metal, glass, plastic or fibre. Glass may be very hard and stiff, but if it is bent too much, it cracks and shatters. Plastic can bend much more easily, but it is not very hard. Add the two together and the resulting composite, glass-reinforced plastic, has the main benefits of both its ingredients. Composites are purpose-made for special uses, by mixing ingredients in certain proportions.

Based on carbon

Many composites are based on the element (pure chemical substance) carbon. An atom of carbon has four available links, to join or bond with up to four other atoms. What makes carbon special is that it links easily to itself, forming long chains, circles, pyramids and even spheres all made out of carbon atoms.

Composite blades

A wind generator turns the kinetic energy of moving air into electricity. Its blades or rotors must have the right amount of flexibility. Too stiff, and they would snap in a powerful wind. Too bendy, and they might kink or crack. So they are made from a specially designed composite, such as carbon-fibre plastic.

Carbon-fibre composite

Carbon fibres are black, silky strands of pure carbon, with the atoms linked together into long chains. They resist the stresses of being pulled or stretched much better than steel. Carbon-fibre composites have hundreds of uses – from powerboat hulls, and the parts for racing cars, to tennis racquets.

Designing composites

Each composite is made as a prototype or test material, where scientists make an informed guess about the proportions of the different ingredients.

Metal

The grains or crystals of a metal give hardness to the composite. They also help to carry electricity. The more metal in a composite, the better it becomes as an electrical conductor.

Composite composites

The streamlined bodywork of a racing car contains a mix of glass-fibres and carbon-fibres in plastic resins.

Fibre

Hair-like fibres or filaments give flexibility to the composite, without allowing it to crack or snap. There are many kinds of fibres, made from carbon, plastic or even glass.

The composite

All the ingredients are brought together in combination. The way the fibres are arranged will affect whether the composite has bending strength in just one direction, or several directions. The ingredients may be spread through, or embedded in, a surrounding 'background' substance called a matrix. Plastics and resins are common as matrix materials.

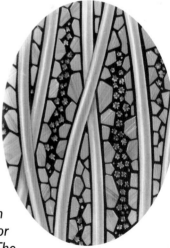

Ceramic

Ceramics are clay-based materials that are very hard, and also withstand great heat and chemicals. Tiny particles of ceramic make a composite tougher and less prone to overheating.

GLASS

Liquid or solid?

Glass is difficult, not only to see, but also to describe. As a 'supercooled liquid', glass is like a clear liquid, similar to water, which has cooled enough to become almost solid. However, it cannot flow like water. Another description is 'amorphous solid', which refers to the lack of any patterns or structures in glass, on the microscopic or molecular scale. This absence of internal structure is one reason why glass cracks at almost any site and any angle.

Making glass

Here people are manufacturing a glass telecope. Most glass is made from the minerals silica (silicon dioxide, SiO_2, which makes up sand), sodium-containing soda ash, and calcium-containing limestone. These are heated in a furnace to about 1500°C. They melt and mix, and are then cooled.

The first telescopes

Telescopes were probably invented in the Netherlands around 1600–1608. The first eminent scientist to study the night sky through a telescope was Italian physicist Galileo Galilei (1564–1642). By 1610 he had written descriptions of craters on the Moon, many stars too faint to see with the unaided eye, and also tiny moons orbiting the planet Jupiter. This last discovery showed that not everything in the Universe went around the Earth, as was then believed. It gradually led to a revolution in science.

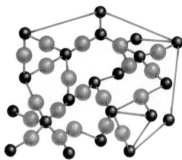

Inside glass

As glassy minerals are heated, they melt and their atoms and molecules are free to move. As they cool they do not have time to take up an ordered, regular pattern. They 'freeze' in random positions as an amorphous solid.

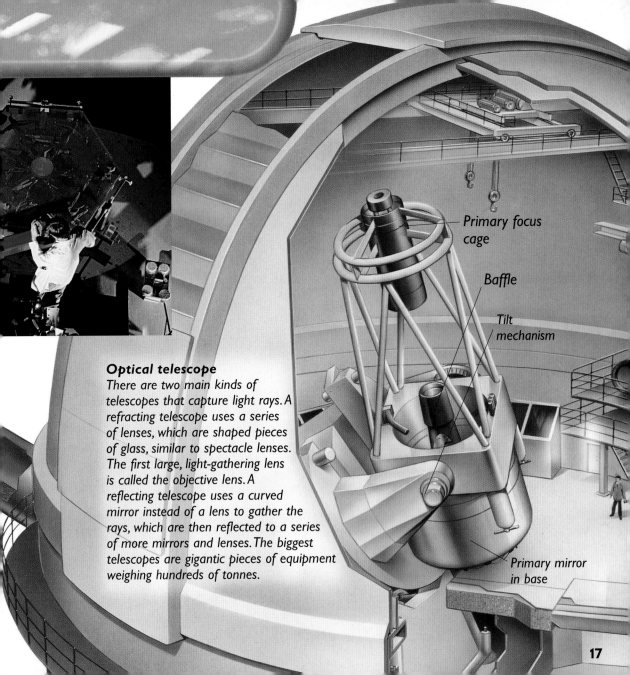

Primary focus cage

Baffle

Tilt mechanism

Optical telescope

There are two main kinds of telescopes that capture light rays. A refracting telescope uses a series of lenses, which are shaped pieces of glass, similar to spectacle lenses. The first large, light-gathering lens is called the objective lens. A reflecting telescope uses a curved mirror instead of a lens to gather the rays, which are then reflected to a series of more mirrors and lenses. The biggest telescopes are gigantic pieces of equipment weighing hundreds of tonnes.

Primary mirror in base

METALS

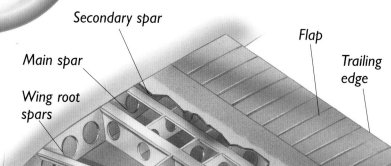

Secondary spar

Main spar

Wing root spars

Rib

Leading edge

Flap

Trailing edge

Aileron

Metal wing
The wing of a plane is curved on top and flat below. This shape, the aerofoil section, provides a lifting force as it moves through the air. The wing has many internal parts, mostly alloys of aluminium.

A world of metals
There are 92 naturally-occurring pure substances, or chemical elements. About 60 of these are metals or metal-like. Most metals are strong, hard, tough and shiny when polished, and carry heat and electricity well. We use several metals in huge amounts. Aluminium is strong but very light and is used in aircraft. Copper carries electricity well and is found in wires and cables. The metal iron is made much harder and stronger by the addition of small amounts of the non-metal element, carbon. The resulting 'mixture', or alloy, is known as steel. It has thousands of uses.

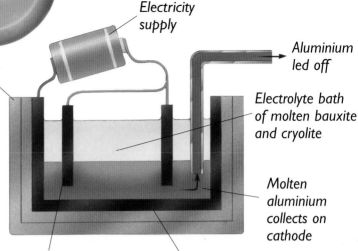

Electricity supply

Aluminium led off

Steel case of electrolytic cell

Electrolyte bath of molten bauxite and cryolite

Purifying metals
Some metals are purified by electrolysis. Aluminium is obtained from its main ore, bauxite, which is processed and heated to 900°C with another substance, cryolite. An enormous electric current passes through the mixture between two graphite electrodes. Aluminium collects at the negative electrode in molten form.

Molten aluminium collects on cathode

Graphite anode (positive electrode rod)

Graphite cathode (negative electrode lining cell)

Recycling metals
It takes huge amounts of energy, money and resources to obtain metals from the rocks, or ores, where they naturally occur. Waste, pollution and effort can be saved by recycling metals.

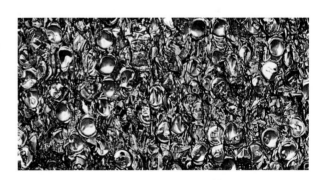

Da Vinci Flyer
Leonardo da Vinci made many designs for flapping-wing aircraft (1480s–1490s) but he lacked light, strong metals such as aluminium.

19

LIQUIDS

Go with the flow

Water changes shape as it flows from one place to another. So do oil, alcohol and petrol. These are all liquids. A liquid, like a gas, is a fluid. It can move, spread out under the downward pull of gravity, and change shape to fit its container. But unlike a gas, a liquid does not expand to fill every part of its container. Neither can a liquid be squeezed or compressed as easily as a gas. A liquid tends to remain the same volume.

The fuel tanks of the US Skylab space station (launched in 1973) were made of titanium metal.

Liquid fuel

When a gas changes into a liquid, it takes up much less space – perhaps thousands of times less. So cooling and compressing a gas into liquid is an efficient way of storing it. Many rocket engines carry fuel, or propellant, as a liquid. The tanks that contain the liquid are made of very strong, hard metal, such as titanium, to withstand great temperature and pressure. The liquid changes into gas as it feeds into the engine.

Water on the Moon

There is no liquid water on the Moon, as the Apollo astronauts discovered during their explorations between 1969 and 1972. However, discoveries during the 1990s suggested that there could be water frozen into ice under the surface, actually inside the rocks of the Moon. Since water is vital to life, this raises the possibility that some types of simple life-forms once survived on the Moon.

Lift-off

At the moment of lift-off, the entire space shuttle weighs about 2000 tonnes. Some 710 tonnes are liquid hydrogen and liquid oxygen, intensely cooled and under great pressure in the huge external fuel tank.

The liquid state

A liquid's atoms and molecules are free to move about in relation to each other, but they stay at the same distance apart from each other. So the liquid tends not to expand or contract, unless its temperature changes. As it gets warmer, its atoms and molecules move very slightly farther apart, and also begin to move faster. So the liquid expands slightly, and heat or convection currents are set up within it, which spread out the heat energy.

Weightless liquid

On the surface of the Earth, the force of gravity pulls a liquid downwards. In the weightless conditions of space, it floats freely. Without the one-sided pull of gravity, each drop forms a perfect sphere.

PLASMA

Hot and electric

The three familiar states of matter are solid, liquid and gas. But there is a fourth state – plasma. It usually occurs only at very high temperatures, generally thousands of degrees Celsius. A plasma is an ionized gas – a gas that contains ions. This means it is a gas in which the atoms, which normally have no electric charge, have become ions, which do have an electric charge, either positive or negative. Ions occur much more commonly in liquids. When a substance, such as sodium chloride (common salt) dissolves, it forms positive sodium ions and negative chloride ions.

Where plasmas are found
Temperatures high enough to form plasmas are found under special conditions on Earth, both natural and man-made, and also in various places in space, such as inside stars. One example is the auroras called the Northern and Southern Lights, which are vast, glowing, rippling curtains of light high in the sky, near the North and South Poles. A sudden flash of lightning can also heat the air next to it to form plasma for a split second.

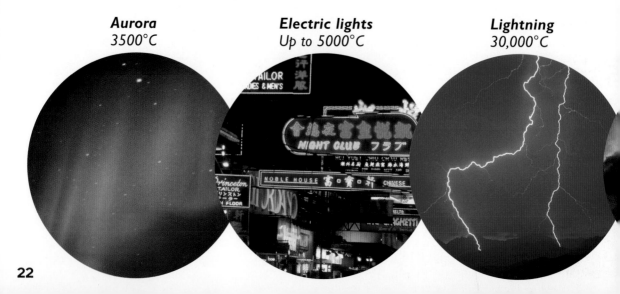

Aurora
3500°C

Electric lights
Up to 5000°C

Lightning
30,000°C

The fourth state of matter

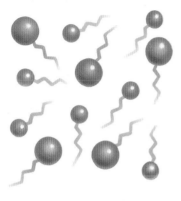

Plasma consists of atoms that move very fast indeed, and freely, as in a gas, to fill up the space they are allowed. However the atoms have lost or gained particles called electrons. Atoms that lose electrons become positive and those that gain electrons become negative. These electrically charged versions of atoms are known as ions.

Power from plasma

Normal nuclear power is obtained by fission, which is splitting the nuclei (centres) of atoms. Another possibility is fusion, where nuclei are pressed together so that they fuse or join. Plasma fusion power (above) is being researched, but the practical problems are huge. The plasma fuel must be heated so much that it cannot be kept in place by a container because its walls would melt. It has to be confined by intense magnetism, which uses more energy than is obtained from fusion in the plasma.

Nebula
25,000 to 50,000°C

Sun's corona

6000°C

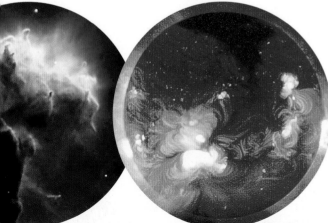

GASES

Vital but invisible

There are gases all around us. If there were not, we would die. Air is a mixture of several invisible gases. The main one is nitrogen, which makes up about four-fifths of air. Next is oxygen, which is vital for our bodily life processes, and which we take in by breathing. There are also small amounts of other gases, including argon, carbon dioxide, neon, helium, krypton, xenon and ozone.

The gaseous state
Like a liquid, a gas 'flows'. Its atoms or molecules can move about freely at high speed. However, they are much farther apart and travel much faster, in a gas than in a liquid. Given more space, they spread out even farther.

Compressing air

As a gas is forced into a smaller container, its atoms or molecules become closer together, and the pressure of the gas rises. The atoms also bump into each other more often, so the temperature rises, too. Air is compressed like this when it is pumped into a tyre, which is why the tyre becomes hot.

Gas fuels

Some gases are made of molecules that contain plenty of chemical energy in the bonds between their atoms. Examples include methane (CH_4), ethane (C_2H_6) and propane (C_3H_8). These are burned as fuels for engines and heating. They are compressed so much, for storage in tanks (right), that they turn from gas into liquid.

Emergency

If an aircraft leaks, its gases rapidly flow away and the plane 'depressurizes'. An emergency system provides vital oxygen from cylinders for breathing through masks.

Extra back-up oxygen cylinders

Oxygen pipes

Oxygen cylinders

Life-saving gas

As you travel higher, away from the Earth's surface, the air becomes thinner with less oxygen, colder, and lower in pressure. These conditions would be dangerous for the human body, so planes are sealed airtight with the correct oxygen content, temperature and pressure inside.

Life-threatening gas

Hydrogen, a flammable gas, was once used to keep airships afloat. However, in 1937 the hydrogen in the airship Hindenburg ignited, killing many of the ship's passengers. Helium is now used as it is non-flammable.

SOLIDS

Unchanging shapes

A substance that stays the same shape, and does not alter or flow, is a solid. Its atoms are arranged in a certain pattern, and hardly move about in relation to each other. Some solids are very hard and tough, such as most metals and rocks. Others can change shape when squeezed or stretched, such as rubber and elastic. However, they do not spread out and flow from place to place, like a liquid or gas.

Crystals

In some solids, the atoms have a pattern or arrangement that repeats itself many times, like bricks in a wall. The larger the solid object, the more of these repeating units it contains. This structure gives the whole solid object a certain shape, with flat sides or faces, and sharp edges. These types of solid are called crystals.

Laser light

A source of energy, such as ordinary light from a flash tube, is fed into an active medium – a crystal such as ruby. As more energy is 'pumped' in, the energy levels rise in the atoms. Suddenly all the atoms give out excess energy as a flash of laser light.

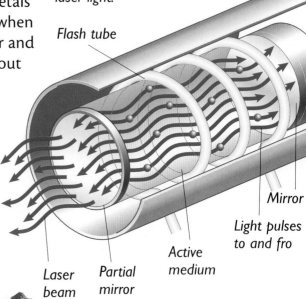

Flash tube

Mirror

Light pulses to and fro

Laser beam

Partial mirror

Active medium

Quartz

Galena

Pyrite

Gypsum

Barite

Calcite

Colours of solids

For objects that do not make their own light, such as guitars, loudspeakers and performers, their colour depends on the colours of light that they absorb. The solid surface of the loudspeaker absorbs all the light that falls on it, and reflects very little, which is why it is black.

The solid state

The wood of a guitar, its metal strings and its plastic trim are all types of solid. The atoms in a solid are close together, fixed in position by chemical bonds and other forces. Each one can move or vibrate slightly around a central point – its 'average' position.

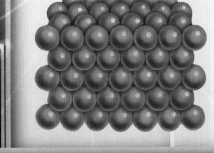

A new kind of light

American scientist Theodore Maiman (1927–) made the first working laser in 1960. He used a rod-shaped ruby crystal that produced red light. Laser light differs from ordinary light in three ways. First, its beam does not spread out or disperse. Second, all its waves are the same length, and so the same pure colour. Third, all the waves are in step, their peaks in line. These features give laser light great power.

PARTICLES

Smaller and smaller

What makes up the Universe? What does matter – from a grain of sand, to the human body – consist of? One idea was that all matter contained tiny building-blocks called atoms. They were the smallest particles, and could not be split further. However, in the early 20th century, atoms were split. They were made of even smaller particles, chiefly protons, neutrons and electrons. In the middle of the 20th century it became clear that some of these sub-atomic particles were composed of yet smaller particles, such as quarks. How do we know? We blast apart these tiny objects in particle-accelerators or 'atom-smashers'.

Detector
Particles collide or smash together in detectors, which are like giant, fast-action electronic cameras.

Bits and pieces

The two main groups of fundamental particles are quarks and leptons. There are six kinds or 'flavours' of quarks – up, down, bottom, top, strange and charm. A proton is two up and one down quarks; a neutron is one up and two down quarks. The six kinds of leptons include the electron.

CERN
This accelerator under the Swiss–French border has a tunnel 27 km in length.

leptons

quarks

Aerial view of the CERN ring-shaped particle accelerator

Electromagnets

These are switched on and off to give extra energy to the particles inside their tubes.

Big rings

The largest particle accelerators are by far the world's biggest machines – huge tunnels usually underground. The particles are given off by very hot, electrified filaments of metals and other substances. The ring structure means the particles can go round and round, faster every time, until diverted by more magnets into the detectors.

Tunnel structure

An accelerator usually has two tunnels, one inside the other. The inner tunnel has no air – it is a vacuum so the particles can move at maximum speed.

Small idea

The idea of all matter being made of tiny particles goes back to Ancient Greece. The thinker Democritus (who lived about 470–400 BC) suggested that the Universe was a vast area of nothing, with atoms scattered about. He believed that each atom was too small to see, too hard to split or break, and lasted forever.

ELECTRONS

Electrons and microchips
A microchip is a thin wafer or sliver of germanium, silicon or a similar element that may or may not conduct electrons, depending on the conditions. Such elements are known as semiconductors. Micro-components are formed on the semiconductor and linked to create circuits.

Atoms and electrons

The smallest chemical units of matter are atoms. Once an atom of a chemical element is split apart, its sub-atomic particles no longer have the properties of the original element. In fact, each type of sub-atomic particle is the same in all atoms. Electrons in a carbon atom are the same as electrons in atoms of iron, aluminium, sulphur, sodium and all other elements – likewise for the protons and the neutrons. Electrons are especially important sub–atomic particles because they can 'hop' from one atom to another, forming an electric current. They can also pass through air or a vacuum as electron beams.

Electronic circuits
In a typical piece of electrical equipment, microchips, resistors, capacitors and other components are joined by wires to form circuits that manipulate electrons and thus electric currents. The metal wires and strips that connect the components are put onto a non-conducting baseboard by a process that is similar to printing inks onto paper. The boards are known as printed circuit boards.

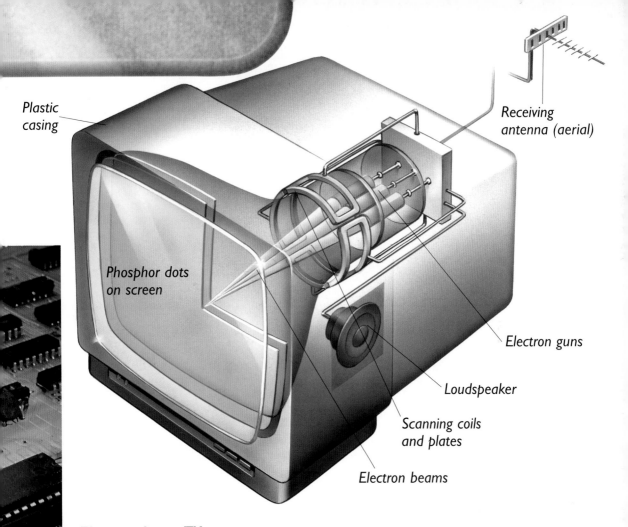

Plastic
casing

Receiving
antenna (aerial)

Phosphor dots
on screen

Electron guns

Loudspeaker

Scanning coils
and plates

Electron beams

Electron beam TV

In a TV set, streams of electron particles are fired from 'guns' by very high-voltage
bursts of electricity. The electrons pass through the vacuum inside the shaped glass
container, or TV tube, to hit the screen at the front. The inside of the screen is coated
with tiny coloured dots of the substance phosphor, which glow when hit by electrons.
As the beams scan to and fro across the screen, many times each second, they build
up a series of still images that our eyes merge into moving pictures.

ELEMENTS

Elements in DNA

The substance DNA (de-oxyribonucleic acid), which carries the body's genetic instructions, is made of millions of atoms. These are made from only five elements – carbon, hydrogen, oxygen, nitrogen and phosphorus. The atoms are arranged in subgroups and strung together as two long 'backbones' twisted around each other, with cross-links between the backbones.

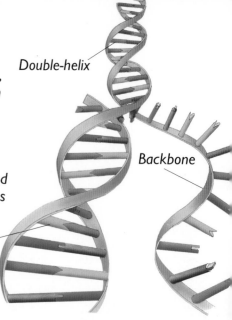

Double-helix

Backbone

Information coded in sequences of cross-links

The number of elements

There are 92 elements that occur naturally, and another 25 that have been created artificially by scientists. They vary from soft white metals such as calcium, to hard, dense metals such as iron. Under the microscope, some resemble fibres or strings, while others are jagged-edged crystals.

Same and different

Although there are trillions of atoms, only a few different kinds of atom exist. Each kind has a certain number of protons and neutrons in its nucleus, with a certain number of electrons going around the nucleus. These atom 'types' are known as chemical elements. Examples of elements include carbon, oxygen, nitrogen, iron, sulphur, chlorine, sodium and gold. All atoms of an element, such as carbon, are the same as each other, and different from the atoms of all other elements.

Elements in the body

The most common elements in the body, by weight, are the most common elements in most biochemicals – oxygen, carbon and hydrogen. Molecules made from atoms of these three elements alone are known as carbohydrates. The element calcium is an important part of teeth and bones, giving strength and toughness.

1 Oxygen 65%
2 Carbon 18.5%
3 Hydrogen 9.5%
4 Nitrogen 3.2%
5 Calcium 1.5%
6 Others 2.3%

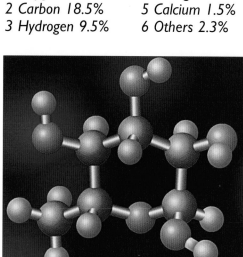

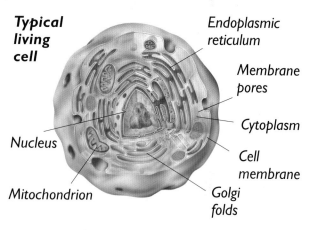

Typical living cell

Endoplasmic reticulum

Membrane pores

Cytoplasm

Cell membrane

Golgi folds

Mitochondrion

Nucleus

Energy for cells

The major energy source for cells needed to power their life processes, is the sugar molecule, glucose. This is a carbohydrate made of only 24 atoms from three elements – carbon, hydrogen and oxygen ($C_6H_{12}O_6$).

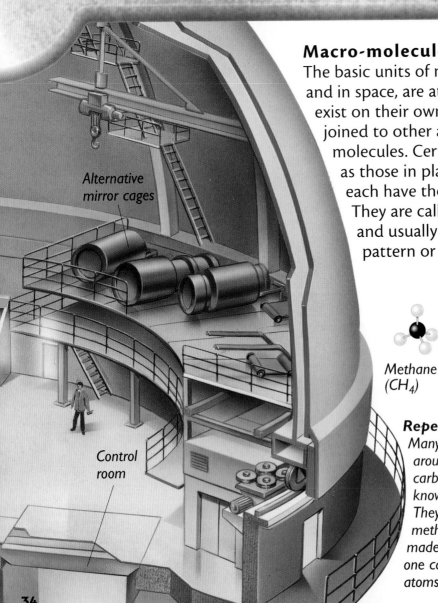

Alternative
mirror cages

Control
room

Macro-molecules

The basic units of matter, both on Earth and in space, are atoms, but they rarely exist on their own. They are usually joined to other atoms to form molecules. Certain molecules, such as those in plastics and proteins, each have thousands of atoms. They are called macro-molecules, and usually have a regular pattern or repeating structure.

Methane
(CH_4)

Butane
(CH_3-CH_3)

Ethene
(CH_2=CH_2)

Repeating structure

Many macro-molecules are built around the two elements of carbon and oxygen, and are known as organic hydrocarbons. They include gases such as methane and butane. Some are made up of repeating units of one carbon and two hydrogen atoms, -CH_2- .

Bright and hot

The H-R (Hertzsprung-Russell) diagram is a graph that compares the brightness of stars with their colours. The colour of a star shows its temperature – cooler stars are red, medium-hot ones are yellow, and very hot stars are white or blue. Most stars form a line on the chart called the Main Sequence. Red giant stars and white dwarf stars form separate groups.

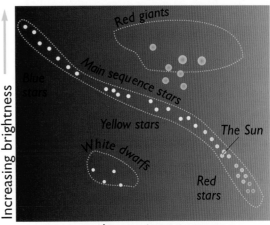

Increasing brightness → *Increasing temperature*

Red giants
Blue stars
Main sequence stars
Yellow stars
The Sun
White dwarfs
Red stars

Molecules from space

How did life begin on Earth? One idea was that life did not start here. Simple life-forms appeared somewhere else in the Universe, and travelled to Earth on a long-distance space wanderer, such as a comet or asteroid.

Martian molecules

In the early 1990s scientists studied a meteorite that came from Mars. The microscope revealed tiny sausage-like shapes, each hundreds of times thinner than a human hair. One explanation was that they were micro-fossils – preserved remains of microbes. This meant that there could be life on Mars! Another explanation was that they were minerals created by natural rock-forming processes.

STORING ELECTRICITY

Power station

Energy to make electricity
Various sources of energy can be converted into electricity. The most common form is chemical energy, in fuels such as coal, oil (petroleum), natural gas and wood. This is burned to form heat energy, which spins turbines as kinetic energy (movement), which is finally converted by a generator into electrical energy.

Moving electrons
Current electricity exists as moving electrons, which are particles normally found in the outer parts of atoms. In certain substances, especially metals, the outermost electrons can detach easily from their atoms. They jump to nearby atoms. Billions of electrons all hopping in the same direction, from atom to atom, create an electric current.

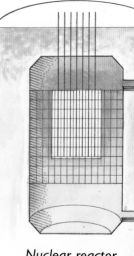

Nuclear reactor

Insulating plastic cover

Plastic coating
Wires and cables are coated with plastic insulation. This plastic coating protects the wire and is also flexible enough to allow the wire to be bent into any shape.

Nuclear power
Heat is given off as the nuclei (centres) of atoms break apart.

Current electricity

Static electricity is like water held behind a dam, ready to flow somewhere. Electricity that moves or flows along, like water in a river, is known as current electricity. It is a very powerful and adaptable form of energy. One of its main features is that it can be transported from place to place, by sending it along wires or cables. Also it can be changed or converted into many other forms of energy, including sound, light and heat.

Alternating current

The electricity made by power stations is alternating current, AC. The direction of the current goes one way, then flows the other way, then reverses again, and so on.

Transmitting electricity

The electricity made by the generator is carried through cables called power lines. They are buried underground or held up on tall towers, for safety.

Transforming electricity

Before feeding electric current to the main power lines, its voltage (pushing strength) is boosted to hundreds of thousands of volts, by a device called a transformer. This allows the current to travel long distances along power lines without losing too much of its energy, especially as heat.

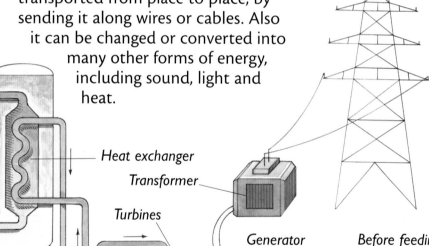

Heat exchanger

Transformer

Turbines

Generator

Secondary circuit of hot water

ELECTRICAL SIGNALS

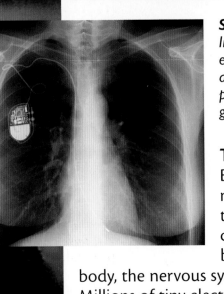

Signals to the heart
In some heart problems, the impulses of electricity that control the heart's beating are not produced properly. So an artificial pacemaker may be put under the skin to generate electrical signals for the heart.

The electric body
Electricity can be converted into many other forms of energy – and the reverse. An example of these conversions at work is the human body. In fact, a major system of the body, the nervous system, is based on electricity. Millions of tiny electrical pulses pass along the network of nerves that branches through all body parts, and also to, from and within the brain. The pulses are termed nerve signals or nervous impulses and they represent thoughts, memories and sensations.

Axon terminal

Electrical cell
The nerve cell or neurone is specialized to pass on nerve signals. It receives signals from other cells through its short, branched dendrites, which may number many thousand. The signals pass through the long, wire-like axon and are then transmitted to other cells.

Whole body scan (left)

Passing on electro-signals

A nerve cell is separated from other nerve cells by tiny gaps known as synapses. When a nerve signal reaches a synapse, it converts to chemical form – biochemicals called neurotransmitters. These cross the synapse in a split second and generate a nerve signal in the receiving cell.

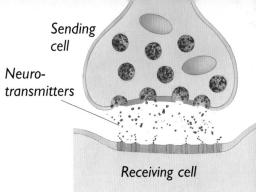

Sending cell

Neuro-transmitters

Receiving cell

Seeing nerve signals

Delicate medical equipment can detect the tiny electrical pulses of nerve signals, or their effects, and strengthen them enough to display on a screen or paper strip. The pulses are usually picked up by sensors placed on the skin.

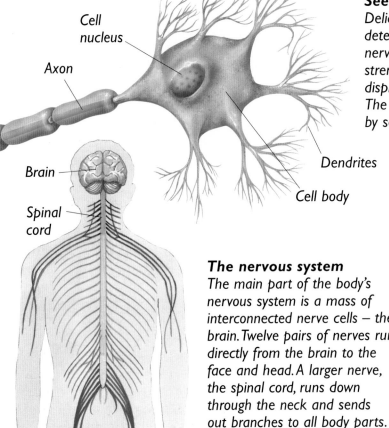

Cell nucleus

Axon

Brain

Spinal cord

Dendrites

Cell body

The nervous system

The main part of the body's nervous system is a mass of interconnected nerve cells – the brain. Twelve pairs of nerves run directly from the brain to the face and head. A larger nerve, the spinal cord, runs down through the neck and sends out branches to all body parts.

CONDUCTING ELECTRICITY

Electron

Atom

Electron hops
to next atom

Units

The pushing strength of an electric current is known as potential difference and is measured in volts. It is like the pressure of water flowing through a pipe. The quantity of electricity is called its current and is measured in amps. Any obstacle or narrow part that the electricity tries to pass is known as resistance, and is measured in ohms.

Current – amps

Potential difference – volts

Resistance – ohms

In a wire

Substances that carry electricity well are known as conductors. Most metals are good conductors. They have atoms with just one or two outermost electrons. These can easily detach from their atom and jump to the next one. When millions of electrons do this, their flow is an electric current.

Transforme

To the home

Electricity arrives in a neighbourhood along huge power lines that carry hundreds of thousands of volts. Before use, the voltage is lowered, or stepped down, by devices known as transformers.

Push and power

Water flowing in a river can be measured in several ways. Quantity is the amount of water flowing past one place over a certain time. Pressure is the pushing force of the water. Electricity is similar to water in the way it is measured. It has a pushing force, a rate of flow, and other features that can be measured. This is vital when planning electrical equipment, from a small microchip to the distribution grid for a whole country.

Electron in outermost shell

Metal atom

Like most metals, uranium carries electricity well. Each of its atoms (above) has lots of electrons, but only two in its outermost layer or shell. These can move fairly easily and as they hop from one uranium atom to another, they form an electric current.

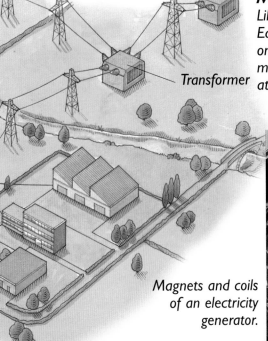

Transformer

Magnets and coils of an electricity generator.

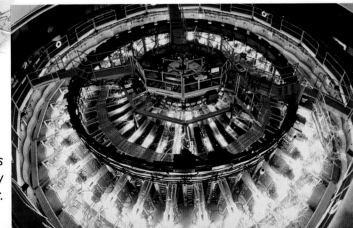

Manipulating

Electricity is a useful form of energy, partly because it can be altered and manipulated in many ways, by a range of electrical devices and electronic components. A capacitor stores electric charge. A resistor makes the flow of electricity weaker. An amplifier makes it stronger. An electric current can flow steadily in one direction, which is DC, or direct current. Or it can flow one way, then the other, then the first way, and so on, reversing 50 or 60 times each second. This is AC, or alternating current.

Effects of static

There are two kinds of electrostatic charge – positive and negative. Like charges repel, unlike ones attract. If like charges build up on objects, including hair, they repel each other, causing a hair-raising effect.

Moving and still

Electricity flows along a wire as electrodynamic charge. If it has nowhere to flow, it collects on the surface of an object as electrostatic charge (static electricity). Van de Graaff generators (left) build up charges of millions of volts, which finally leap away as giant sparks.

Transistor

Battery current flows through these two layers

Bigger

A microphone produces tiny electrical pulses that vary with the sounds it receives. These signals are not strong enough to power a loudspeaker. But as the signals pass through a transistor, they can manipulate the much stronger electricity from a battery, in the same pattern as themselves. The increased or amplified signals then drive the loudspeaker.

Microphone signals flow through these two layers

Loudspeaker

Larger electrical signals from battery

Replica of an early transistor (1947)

Tiny electrical signals from microphone

Stronger electricity

An amplifier is a device which amplifies, or strengthens, electrical signals. It is the electronic version of a mechanical lever. It takes a series of small electrical signals and uses these to control a larger electric current. The smaller set of signals manipulates the larger current to make the same pattern of signals, but greater in strength.

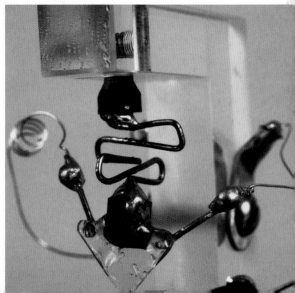

BIOCHEMICALS

Living chemical factories

A living thing, such as the human body, is a vast collection of millions of chemicals, which are changing and reacting all the time. Substances that are found particularly in living things are termed biochemicals, and many of them are the same throughout the living world. For example, plants make the sugar glucose as they trap light energy from the Sun by photosynthesis. Almost all animals, including humans, use glucose too, as a source of energy called 'blood sugar'.

Clear fluid in eyeball

Retina

Optic nerve

Sheath of eyeball

Lens

Cornea

Light and bio-change

Light shines onto a very thin layer inside the back of the eyeball called the retina. Each of the 125 million cells in the retina contains millions of copies of the bio-molecule rhodopsin. When light hits rhodopsin, it causes the rhodopsin to change shape, and this in turn generates a nerve pulse that passes to the brain.

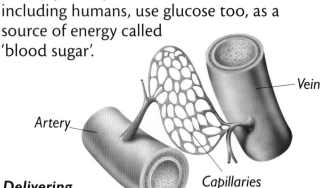

Vein

Artery

Capillaries

Delivering biochemicals

Arteries convey blood from the heart to every region. The arteries branch and divide many times until they are thinner than hairs, and known as capillaries. Glucose, oxygen and other vital biochemicals pass through the very thin walls of the capillaries to the body's tissues and cells. The capillaries join to form wide veins, which return the blood to the heart.

The ultimate biochemical

The instructions for how the body grows and develops, called genes, are in the form of biochemicals. They are known as DNA (de-oxyribonucleic acid). A molecule of DNA has a corkscrew-like shape, called the double-helix.

Storing biochemicals

The largest organ (major part) inside the body is the liver. It stores many vital substances including vitamins and minerals. It also stores spare glucose from food by linking many molecules of it into a much larger bio-molecule, starch. If the body suddenly needs extra energy, the liver changes some of its starch into glucose and releases this into the blood stream.

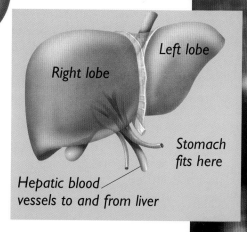

Left lobe

Right lobe

Stomach fits here

Hepatic blood vessels to and from liver

Red blood cells

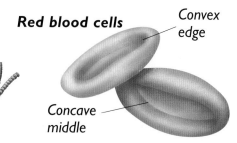

Convex edge

Concave middle

Oxygen and biochemicals

Oxygen is absorbed through the lungs into the blood. For transport, it attaches to an iron-containing biochemical called haemoglobin, which is contained in red blood cells. There are five million red cells in a pinhead-sized drop of blood, and 270 million molecules of haemoglobin in each red cell. Away from the lungs, where levels of oxygen are lower, haemoglobin releases its oxygen for the cells and tissues.

Speeding up bio-reactions

Substances called catalysts can speed up or slow down chemical changes. The catalysts found in living things are called enzymes. The first person to make the pure form of an enzyme and study it was German bio-scientist Theodore Schwann (1810–1882) in about 1835. The enzyme is called pepsin. In the stomach it speeds up the breakdown and digestion of proteins in food.

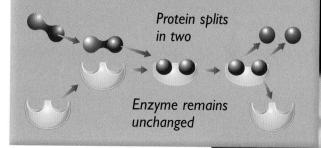

Protein splits in two

Enzyme remains unchanged

CATALYSTS

Faster or slower

When two chemicals come together and change, or react, they do so at a certain rate. This depends partly on the nature of the chemicals themselves, and also on conditions, such as temperature and pressure. However, the rate of reaction can be altered by another substance, called a catalyst. This 'helps' the reaction and may take part in it. But at the end, the catalyst has not been altered, and is the same as at the start.

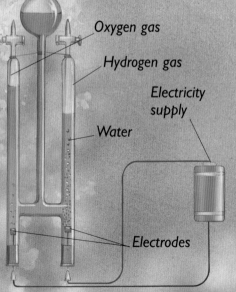

Oxygen gas

Hydrogen gas

Electricity supply

Water

Electrodes

Making air

A submarine stays underwater for months. Chemical systems on board refresh the air. Catalysts remove dangerous gases such as carbon dioxide and carbon monoxide. Vital oxygen is made by electrolysis – passing electricity through a liquid such as water, to split its molecules and release oxygen as a gas for breathing.

Catalysts in fuel

Various catalysts are added to fuels, such as the rocket fuel in submarine-launched missiles. Some catalysts make the fuel reach full burning power very quickly. Others help the rocket engine to fire smoothly, without surges. The used or spent catalyst is blasted out of the rocket, along with the hot gases from the burn.

Fresh water from salty

Salty water can be changed into fresh by desalination. Sea water is heated and the water vapour given off is collected and condensed – cooled back into liquid pure water – leaving salt behind. In practice, partly-heated sea water is passed through a low-pressure chamber, where the water boils at a lower temperature, lessening the need for heat energy. Desalination is used in submarines and in towns along the coasts of desert regions.

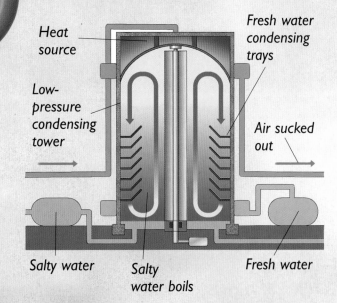

Heat source

Fresh water condensing trays

Low-pressure condensing tower

Air sucked out

Salty water

Salty water boils

Fresh water

Torpedo

The torpedo is a long, slim, self-powered weapon that races through the water towards an enemy target. One type has an explosive warhead near the front, a central control section, batteries and an electric motor that spins the screws (propellers) at the rear. Sonar sensors at the front detect the sounds of an enemy vessel, and the torpedo adjusts its path so that the sounds become louder, until it reaches the target.

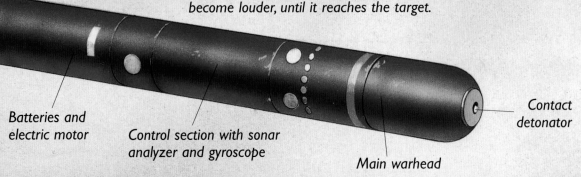

Batteries and electric motor

Control section with sonar analyzer and gyroscope

Main warhead

Contact detonator

COMBUSTION

Burns and blow-ups

Combustion is a special kind of chemical change. It is the rapid combination of a substance with oxygen. Some of the energy in the chemical bonds of the substance is changed into heat and light, and the substance itself is drastically changed. Fairly slow combustion is known in everyday terms as burning. The light and heat are given off as flames. An explosion is very sudden, rapid combustion, with plenty of sound energy as well.

Ancient rockets

Gunpowder was one of the earliest substances to combust with explosive force. It was made as a mixture of minerals. Saltpetre (potassium nitrate) provided the oxygen, sulphur caught fire quickly, and powdered charcoal (carbon) burned hot and fiercely. This mixture may have been invented in China, some 1000 years ago, for use in rockets and bombs.

The colours of fireworks are based on different metal-containing chemicals.

Fireworks

A firework rocket uses a modern type of gunpowder-based substance, a solid propellant. This burns very quickly, but not quite with explosive suddenness. The smoke and hot gas products of combustion blast out of the base of the rocket and so thrust it forwards.

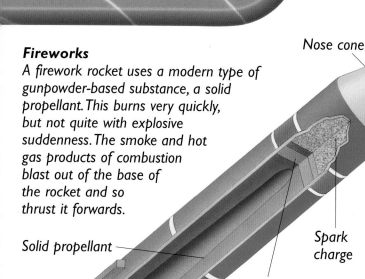

Nose cone

Spark charge

Clay stopper

Solid propellant

Outer casing

Fuse

Launch stick

Burning in air

In an ordinary flame, such as a gas burner, the oxygen comes from the air around. In a rocket or explosion, oxygen is provided by one of the chemicals in the mixture.

Atoms of magnesium, Mg, a silvery metal

Molecule of oxygen, O_2, in air

Atoms join to form magnesium oxide, MgO_2, a white powder

Coloured sparks

The shower of sparks from a firework is produced by combusting metal-containing chemicals with an explosive charge that blows up to spread them out. Magnesium-based chemicals give a very bright white light, while copper chemicals produce green or blue, and sodium gives yellow.

ATOMS

Inside an atom

An atom is made of three main kinds of particles. These are neutrons, protons and electrons. The protons and neutrons are close together in the atom's centre, its nucleus. The electrons move around the nucleus. They do not travel at random, but in certain ball-shaped layers called shells. Electrons in different shells have different amounts of energy. Each pure substance or chemical element has its own number of protons, neutrons and electrons. The number of protons usually equals the number of electrons, and this is called the element's atomic number.

Electron shell M

Electron shell L   Nucleus

Electron shell K

Carbon atom
Nucleus with six protons

Chlorine atom
Nucleus with 17 protons

Oxygen atom
Nucleus with eight protons

Sodium atom
Nucleus with 11 protons

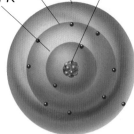

Seven electrons out of eight in shell M means that chlorine is drawn to atoms with a spare electron.

Plus equals minus
In an atom, the number of negative electrons usually balances the number of positive protons, so the whole atom has no charge.

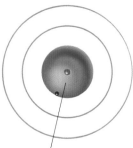

Hydrogen atom
Nucleus with one proton

Single electron

Splitting the atom

The first team of scientists to 'split the atom' was led by New Zealand-born physicist Ernest Rutherford (1871–1937) from about 1919. His early work involved radio waves and radioactivity. In 1911 he suggested that an atom consists of several heavy particles in the middle, with lighter ones moving around them. This was the first correct idea for the structure of an atom.

Ionic bonding

This involves the movement of one or a few electrons in the outermost shell. The electron jumps across to another atom that has a space in its outermost shell. The atom that has lost the negative electron now has a positive charge; the one that gains has a negative charge. When atoms have charges, they are called ions. Ions of different charges, positive and negative, attract and bond to each other.

Shared electrons

Covalent bonding

In this type of bonding an atom, with room in its outermost shell for an extra electron, gains such an electron by 'sharing' it with another atom. The electron repeatedly flips to and fro, first in one atom and then in the other.

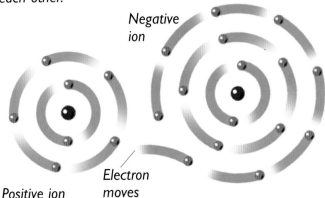

Negative ion

Positive ion

Electron moves

FUEL

Burning fuel

Most types of engine burn fuel. A fuel is a substance that is rich in energy, stored in chemical form as the links between the atoms in its molecules. Common fuels are wood, coal, various gases like methane, propane and butane, and petroleum products such as petrol. When the fuel burns, oxygen combines with its molecules to split them apart. Their chemical energy is converted into heat energy, which is then used by the engine. The process may be continuous, like the roar of a jet engine, or happen in short bursts, like the mini-explosions inside a petrol engine.

Concorde cruised at a speed of 2150 km/h and an altitude of 15,500 m

Jet engine

The main fan sucks in air, which is squeezed by compressor turbines. Fuel burns in the combustion chamber. The hot gases blast out and spin exhaust turbines, which are linked by the shaft to the front turbines.

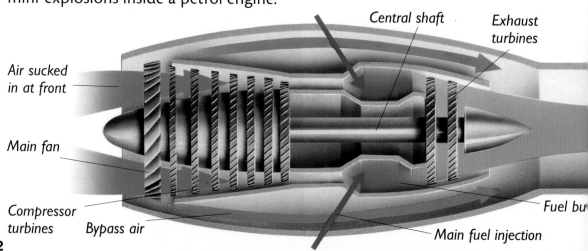

Central shaft

Exhaust turbines

Air sucked in at front

Main fan

Compressor turbines

Bypass air

Fuel bu

Main fuel injection

Petrol, diesel and jet engines
use oxygen to burn their fuels. The oxygen
comes from air, making up about one-fifth of its
volume. As a plane flies higher, air is thinner. This means
less friction from air resistance, but also less oxygen. Above about
25,000 m of altitude, most air-using engines no longer work.

1. INDUCTION
Inlet valve open

2. COMPRESSION
Valves close

3. POWER
Spark and combustion

4. EXHAUST
Exhaust valve open

Valve

Piston

Hot gases
blast out
of rear

Afterburner fuel
injection

Afterburners give
added thrust

Petrol engine
In an internal combustion engine, burning the fuel
takes place in an enclosed space. The standard
petrol engine is 4-stroke: the piston makes four
movements or strokes, up and down twice, for a
complete cycle. The air and fuel mixture enters
through the inlet valve and is set alight by an
electric flash from the spark plug. The sudden small
explosion pushes the piston down with great force.

Rocket engine

A rocket engine works very simply, by burning fuel inside a heat-proof combustion chamber. The hot gases are directed to roar rearwards, out of the exhaust nozzle. Their action, pushing backwards, is accompanied by an equal and opposite reaction, pushing forwards the rocket engine and any objects attached to it. Like any engine that works by combustion, a rocket needs oxygen for its fuel, or propellant, to burn. In the vacuum of space, there is no oxygen. So the rocket takes its own, in the form of an oxidizer – a chemical that breaks down with heat to supply plenty of oxygen.

Early rockets

Apart from early gunpowder rockets, the first modern-style, liquid-fuel rocket flew in 1926. Its fuel was petrol, and its oxidizer was liquid oxygen. Its designer was American scientist Robert Goddard (1882–1945). His first attempt reached a height of about 12 m, but this soon improved. Goddard built bigger, more powerful rockets that sped to heights of 1500 m and travelled faster than sound.

The shuttle set-up

The space shuttle is the world's only re-useable rocket system. The orbiter resembles a plane, with a length of 37.2 m and a wing span of 23.8 m. It has three rocket engines at its rear end. For the first part of the mission these are supplied with propellant and oxidizer by the giant fuel tank, which is 47 m in length. The two boosters have solid fuel and are used only for take-off.

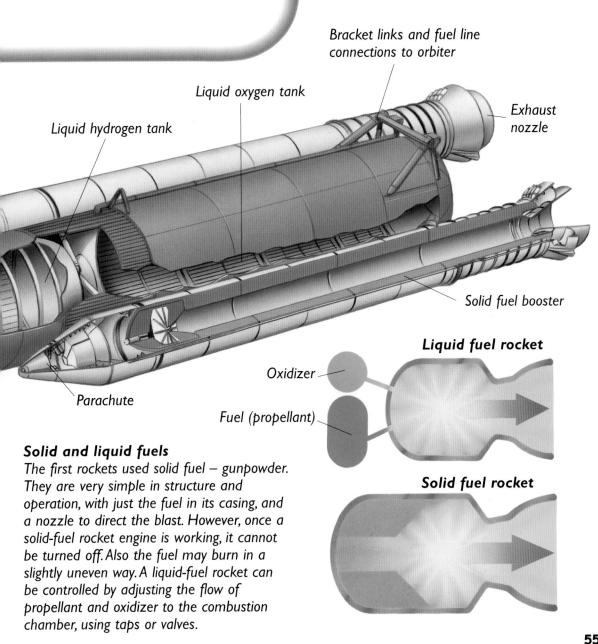

Bracket links and fuel line connections to orbiter

Liquid oxygen tank

Exhaust nozzle

Liquid hydrogen tank

Solid fuel booster

Parachute

Oxidizer

Fuel (propellant)

Liquid fuel rocket

Solid fuel rocket

Solid and liquid fuels
The first rockets used solid fuel – gunpowder. They are very simple in structure and operation, with just the fuel in its casing, and a nozzle to direct the blast. However, once a solid-fuel rocket engine is working, it cannot be turned off. Also the fuel may burn in a slightly uneven way. A liquid-fuel rocket can be controlled by adjusting the flow of propellant and oxidizer to the combustion chamber, using taps or valves.

NUCLEAR ENERGY

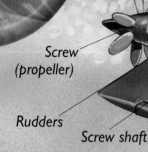

Screw
(propeller)

Rudders

Screw shaft

Main
gearbox

Turbo-generator
for sub's own
electricity supply

Central
shaft

Main
turbines

Back-up diesel
generator

Nuclear reactor

A nuclear reactor uses a fuel, such as
uranium, to produce a controlled chain
reaction of nuclear splitting (fission). This
generates heat, which is then used to spin
turbines and generate electricity. Nuclear
power stations have huge reactors. Smaller
versions are used in submarines, where they
have a great advantage over petrol or diesel
engines – they do not use air.

Nuclear safety

A nuclear reaction produces various
kinds of energy in addition to heat.
Some of this energy is in the form of
harmful radioactivity. Also, if the chain
reaction gets out of control, it may
happen so fast that it causes meltdown
or even a nuclear explosion. So a
nuclear reactor must be protected and
shielded from its surroundings. Different
types of nuclear reactions are tested in
remote areas, like deserts.

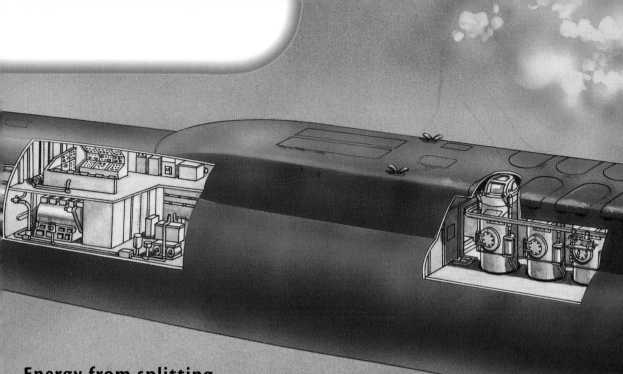

Energy from splitting

All matter is made of tiny pieces called atoms. At the centre of each atom is a nucleus, which is made of two types of sub-atomic particles – protons and neutrons. Certain types of atoms, like uranium, have nuclei which are unstable. These nuclei can be made to break or split, by bombarding them with other particles or energy. As each nucleus splits, some of its particles cease their existence as matter, and turn into energy, chiefly heat.

Atomic clock

Accurate timekeeping by an atomic clock is based on the regular vibrations of atoms.

Detector counts the atoms

Microwave source

Magnet separates atoms

Frequency divider

Digital display

17:00.1070

GENERATORS

Rotor and stator

The main parts of the generator are two huge sets of wire coils, the rotor and stator. The rotor spins inside the stator, which remains stationary.

Contacts

Each sliding electrical contact consists of a metallic strip on the shaft of the generator and a brush that touches it as the shaft rotates. The brush is usually made of a composite material containing carbon, so that it carries electricity but causes little wear or friction. This arrangement is needed to conduct electric current into the fast-spinning coils of the rotor.

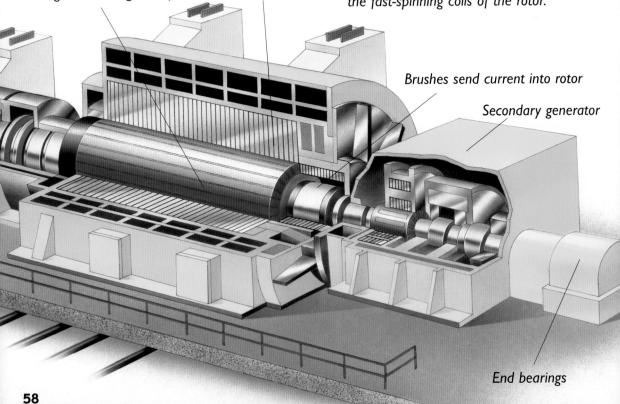

Rotor (spinning coils of wire that use electricity to generate magnetism)

Stator (stationary coils of wire where current is generated)

Brushes send current into rotor

Secondary generator

End bearings

Generators

A generator changes the energy of movement, kinetic energy, into electrical energy. It uses a feature of magnetism and electricity called electromagnetic induction. When a wire moves within a magnetic field, or when a magnetic field moves past a wire, electric current is generated in the wire. In a typical generator, coils of wire spin within powerful magnetic fields, and the electricity generated in them is led away. Electromagnetic induction is the 'opposite' of the electromagnetic effect, where the flow of electricity in a wire produces a magnetic field around the wire.

Solar problems

The Sun's light and heat vary greatly depending on weather and other conditions. They are also very weak in many colder parts of the world, and are absent at night. So solar power has only a limited capacity to generate electricity. Much research continues on industrial methods of storing electricity, in a giant version of a rechargeable car battery, which would help to even out supplies.

Chemical generators

Electricity is generated by chemical reactions in an electrical cell. A group of cells forms a battery. The first battery was developed by Italian scientist Alessandro Volta (1745–1827) in about 1799. It was a pile of alternating silver and zinc discs with card soaked in salt water between them.

Solar power

By far the greatest source of energy near our world is the Sun. Its light and heat can be captured and used to generate electricity in a solar power station.

CIRCULAR MOTION

Kepler and his laws

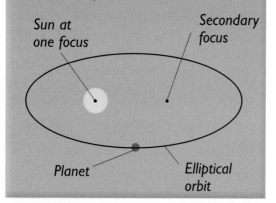

The laws of planetary motion were discovered by German astronomer Johann Kepler between 1608 and 1619. He worked out that Earth and the other planets do not travel in exact circles around the Sun. They move in oval-like shapes called ellipses. The Sun is not in the middle of an orbital ellipse, but at one of its twin 'centres', called a focus. Also each planet does not move at a constant speed. It travels faster as it comes nearer the Sun, then slower as it moves away.

Sun at one focus

Secondary focus

Planet

Elliptical orbit

Round and round

In circular motion, an object stays at a constant distance from one point, the centre, as it moves. This also includes objects that spin or revolve around a central point or line, like a wheel on an axle. The most 'natural' form of movement is actually travelling in a straight line, not circular motion. For an object to travel in a circle, there must be a force on it, which continuously makes its path move around in a curve. For planets orbiting the Sun, the force is the Sun's gravity.

More than half of all stars are not single, like our Sun, but binaries or multiples – two or more stars very close together. Their motions depend on their sizes. Two similar partners follow each other in circular orbit (1). A much smaller star orbits a huge one (2). Or two dissimilar partners orbit a point between them (3).

Solar circles

The Sun is a star in the middle of the Solar System. The system consists of nine planets that orbit in ellipses. The four innermost planets are small and made mainly of rocks. Earth is among them as the 'third rock from the Sun'. After a wide gap populated by even smaller rocks, called asteroids, the next four planets are huge 'gas giants'.

Black hole

A black hole is a place where gigantic amounts of matter are squeezed into an unimaginably small place. Its gravity is so strong and concentrated that nothing can escape – not even light, which is why the hole is black. The gravity pulls planets, stars, gas and dust, which spiral into the hole.

FRICTION

Making heat energy

Friction is 'the enemy of machines'. It changes the energy of motion, kinetic energy, into the energy of heat. Friction is basically rubbing or scraping that causes wear, tear, slowing down and getting hot. No matter how smooth a surface such as polished metal, there are still tiny lumps and bumps, perhaps just a few million atoms high. As another surface slides past, the lumps rub against each other. Friction can be lessened by using very smooth, almost slip-free substances, and with lubrication such as oil or grease.

Low-friction wheels and bearings on rollercoaster

Bicycle brakes

Friction is very useful when used deliberately to slow down motion. Pressing the brake lever makes a cable pull on the brake yokes. These swivel like a pair of levers to make the rubber brake blocks press against the metal rim of the wheel. Water acts as a lubricant and allows the wheel rim to slip past the blocks more easily, which is why bicycle brakes are less effective in wet conditions.

Car brakes

Car brakes work in a similar way to bicycle brakes, but by hydraulics rather than levers. In a car, curved parts called brake shoes press on the drum-shaped inside part of the wheel, to make the wheel spin more slowly. The covering of the brake shoe becomes very hot and so it must be made from a temperature-resistant composite substance.

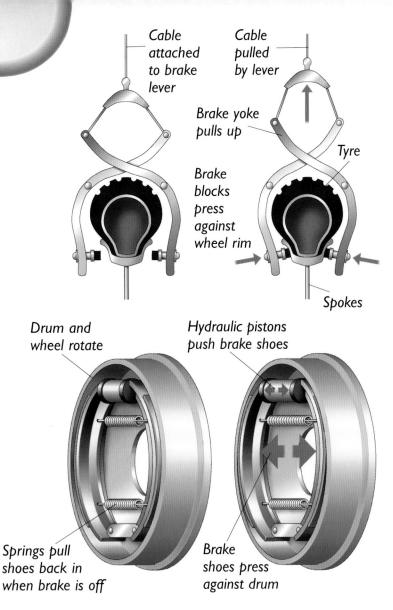

Cable attached to brake lever

Cable pulled by lever

Brake yoke pulls up

Tyre

Brake blocks press against wheel rim

Spokes

Drum and wheel rotate

Hydraulic pistons push brake shoes

Springs pull shoes back in when brake is off

Brake shoes press against drum

ROTARY MOTION

Rotating around

Rotary motion is a special type of circular motion. It happens when an object spins or revolves around a central point or line, like a wheel on an axle, or a set of turbine blades on a shaft. Once a wheel is set turning or rotating, it has a tendency to keep turning – a feature known as angular momentum. The heavier the wheel and objects connected to it, the greater the momentum. This effect is used in massive flywheels, which are used to smooth out small fluctuations in rotational speed.

Spin and shake

A modern generator in a power station is a gigantic machine that runs for years without stopping and with hardly any maintenance. Its rotating parts have to be perfectly balanced in their bearings. Otherwise, as they spin, they would set up vibrations that cause wear, and might eventually create cracks or even shake the device apart. The forces that affect spinning objects are very different from those that put stress on stationary objects.

New water turbines

The modern hydro-electric turbine is an electricity-generating version of the old waterwheel. Water held back by a dam is led along pipes to turn angled turbine blades and a generator.

Old water turbines

The waterwheel of ancient times is a type of turbine. Water flows past the angled blades and pushes them, converting the kinetic energy of its flow into the rotational kinetic energy of the wheel. Waterwheels were used for tasks such as turning millstones to grind cereals to flour.

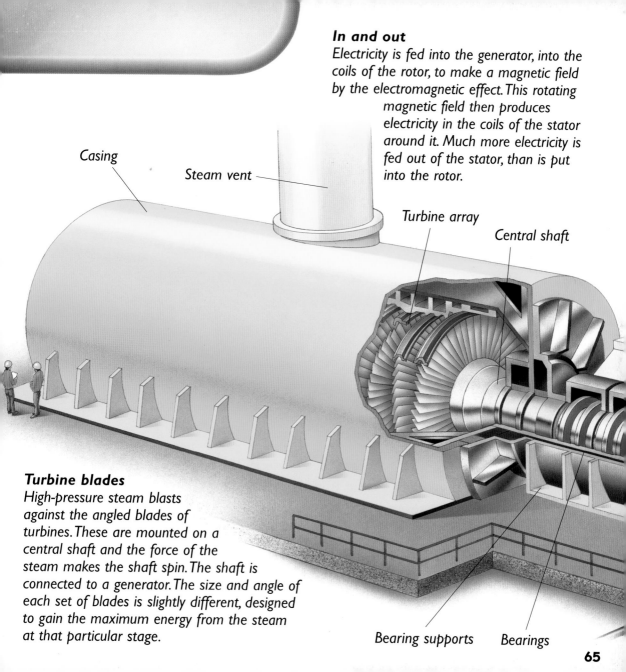

Casing

Steam vent

In and out
Electricity is fed into the generator, into the coils of the rotor, to make a magnetic field by the electromagnetic effect. This rotating magnetic field then produces electricity in the coils of the stator around it. Much more electricity is fed out of the stator, than is put into the rotor.

Turbine array

Central shaft

Turbine blades
High-pressure steam blasts against the angled blades of turbines. These are mounted on a central shaft and the force of the steam makes the shaft spin. The shaft is connected to a generator. The size and angle of each set of blades is slightly different, designed to gain the maximum energy from the steam at that particular stage.

Bearing supports

Bearings

GRAVITY

Everything pulls

Gravity is one of the four fundamental forces of the Universe. It is a pulling or attracting force possessed by all objects, from the particles that make up an atom, to a giant star. Earth's gravity pulls all objects towards it, keeping us and them firmly on the surface. To fly into space, a rocket must get away from the pull of Earth's gravity by moving at a speed called escape velocity, which is 11.2 km/sec.

6

5

Escape of the shuttle

From 3.8 seconds before lift-off (1), all three of the shuttle's orbiter engines fire. The solid-fuel boosters begin their burn 2.9 seconds after lift-off (2). The boosters burn out and release at 2 minutes 12 seconds (3). The external fuel tank is empty and released by 8 minutes 50 seconds (4). The shuttle enters Earth orbit soon after (5) and begins its mission (6).

4

3

2

1

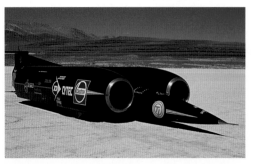

Gravity on land

Super-fast cars like the world land speed record-holder, Thrust SSC, cannot rely on gravity to hold them down. They move so rapidly that they may almost take off. Such cars have aerodynamic shapes to help hold them down.

Gravity, mass and weight

Every object or substance has mass. This is, in effect, a measure of how many atoms, and which types of atoms, it contains. The mass of an object is the same everywhere. A person has the same mass on Earth, in space and on the Moon. Weight is different. It is produced by the pull of gravity acting on the object, and so depends on gravity. A person with a weight of 60 kg on Earth, would weigh about 10 kg on the Moon, and be weightless in the zero-gravity conditions of space.

Earth's gravity

Straight line tendency

Orbital path

Gravity in orbit

Isaac Newton showed that an object tends to keep moving in a straight line, at the same speed, unless a force acts on it. A satellite tries to do this, but the force of Earth's gravity pulls it down. The result is a curved path called an orbit, as the satellite goes round and round the Earth.

Ideas about gravity

English scientist Isaac Newton (1642–1727) suggested that gravity was a universal force, possessed by all objects. Earth's gravity not only pulls falling apples down to the ground, it also holds the Moon in orbit around the Earth. Newton's ideas were revised by Albert Einstein (1879–1955).

GEARS AND COGS

Gears and cogs

Cog wheels have teeth that fit into, or mesh with, similar teeth on another cog wheel. The basic cog wheel set-up can transfer a turning force from one place to another. It can reverse the direction of the turning force, since the driven cog turns in the opposite direction to the driving cog. And depending on the number of teeth, a cog system can speed up or slow down the rate of rotation, and reduce or increase the turning power.

Types of cogs and gears

Cogs or teeth are carefully designed so that they fit very closely, without too much rubbing. This reduces wear and also transfers as much force as smoothly as possible.

Winding mechanism coils spring

Gears on the wrist

A wristwatch gains its energy from a spiral spring that is wound up. The spring's tension is allowed to reduce very slowly by a system of tiny cogs and other gear-type mechanisms. These miniature mechanical devices sometimes have jewelled or diamond bearings, for longevity.

Simple cogs reverse direction of rotation

Rack

Pinion

Bevels move direction of rotation through a right angle (90°)

Worm

Winch

A typical electric winch has a motor that rotates rapidly. A system of gears greatly slows down this turning speed, but at the same time, greatly increases its force. The result is that a rollercoaster car full of people can be winched by a driving cog, meshed into a slotted chain, up a steep slope.

Low and high gears

In low gearing, like the rollercoaster winch, the driving cog turns many times compared to a few turns of the driven cog. But the turning force, or torque, is increased. In a high gear, the opposite occurs. The driven cog rotates very quickly but its torque is decreased.

Winch and gearing mechanism under car

THE WHEEL

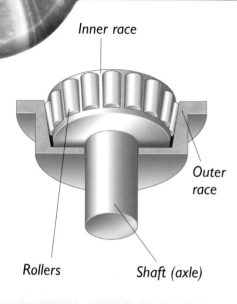

Inner race

Outer race

Rollers

Shaft (axle)

Smooth motion

A bearing is designed to allow one part, such as a wheel, to move against another part, such as an axle, with the least rubbing or friction. The ball-bearing is one of the strongest, most hard-wearing and most effective designs. All the parts are made of hard, smooth metal, usually a type of steel. They are lubricated with grease or oil. A mirror-ball or a spotlight must move smoothly, without jerks, to follow the performers as they travel around the stage, so it is usually mounted on a ball-bearing.

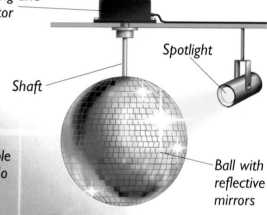

Roller bearing and electric motor

Spotlight

Shaft

Ball with reflective mirrors

Roller-bearing

This bearing is similar to a ball-bearing, but has rollers shaped like rods or cones. The roller-bearing is used for heavier machinery or for bearings that must be long-lasting because they are in inaccessible places. Each roller carries weight along its length. So the pressure is spread out more, compared to a ball-bearing where it is concentrated into spots.

Lots of energy

A stadium show emits many forms of energy – especially sound from the loudspeakers, and light and heat from the lighting system. There are also radio waves from the cordless radio-microphones.

Electric motor

Thousands of machines are driven by electric motors. They are generally quiet, safe, smooth-running, easily controlled and efficent. They change more than nine-tenths of the energy supplied to them as electricity, into the energy of rotary motion.

Rolling and pulling

The wheel is one of the simplest and most common machines. It is like a never-ending inclined plane (slope or ramp) wrapped around a central point, the axle. A wheel reduces the slowing effect of friction hugely, by allowing an object to roll across a surface, rather than being dragged. Wheels do use up some energy, as their edge or rim presses down on the surface. This rolling resistance increases as the wheel's edge, and/or the surface, become less smooth. A pulley is a wheel with a grooved or dished rim. It turns to allow a rope or cable to move past it.

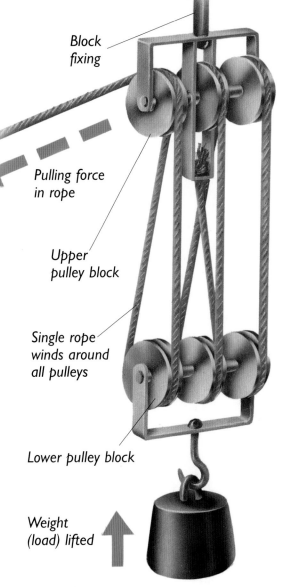

Block fixing

Pulling force in rope

Upper pulley block

Single rope winds around all pulleys

Lower pulley block

Weight (load) lifted

Easing the load

Groups or blocks of pulleys can help to lift heavy loads more easily. One rope or cable passes up and down, around alternate pulleys in the upper and lower blocks. When the rope is wound in, it lifts the load more easily than without pulleys. But more rope has to be wound in, to move the load only a short distance. In this respect, a pulley system is like a lever. A small effort moves a big load, but not very far.

MECHANICAL DEVICES

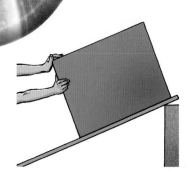

Inclined plane
This is a slope or ramp. It allows an object to be lifted or moved in small, continuous amounts, rather than in one large step.

Wedge
Made of two inclined planes, back to back, the wedge can force two objects apart. Or, in the case of an axe or chisel blade, split an object.

Screw
A wedge, twisted like a corkscrew around a central rod, forms a screw. It converts a turning force into a straight-line movement.

Lever
A rigid bar tilts on a pivot, or fulcrum. A small force at one end produces a large force at the other end.

Wheel and axle
The wheel is like one curved, never-ending inclined plane, wrapped around a central point. It changes sliding or rubbing into rolling.

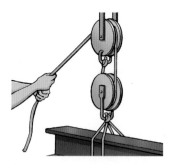

Pulley
A rope or cable passes round a wheel with a dished rim. Pulleys change the direction of a pulling force or convert it to rotary motion.

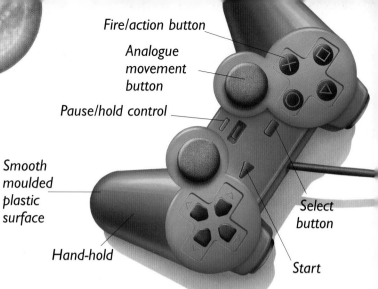

Fire/action button

Analogue movement button

Pause/hold control

Smooth moulded plastic surface

Select button

Hand-hold

Start

Joypad

The switches and buttons are made of plastic and are impact-resistant. They have intricate shapes – features which would be difficult to obtain with other materials, such as wood or glass.

Basic mechanics

Mechanical devices work using physically moving parts, unlike electrical, hydraulic (liquid-based), pneumatic (air), acoustic (sound) or optical (light) systems. Most mechanical devices are built up from combinations of a few very simple machines. These include the inclined plane (ramp), wedge, lever, screw, wheel and axle, and pulley. In daily life, many devices are combinations of these different systems. The handset for a games console has mechanical and electrical components.

Rocker lever

A rocker switch in a joypad works like a lever. The switch is a shaped bar that pivots on its hinge, or fulcrum. There are electrical contacts at one end in the switch and the base. Pressing one end of the switch brings the contacts together so electricity can flow and the switch is ON. Pressing the other end makes the switch flick to OFF.

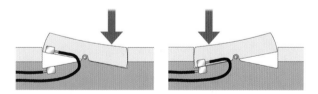

Types of levers

A rocker switch works as two types of lever, depending on the relative positions of the effort (the pressing finger), fulcrum, and load (the contacts). Each type has certain advantages.

HYDRAULIC DEVICES

Liquid pressure

Machines that work using liquids are known
as hydraulic devices. Most liquids cannot be made
smaller, or compressed. So when a liquid is put
under pressure, it transmits the pressure evenly
throughout itself. Push the liquid at one end of a
pipe and the liquid exerts this pressure all along the
walls of the pipe, and at the other end, too.
Hydraulic machines use pipes, pistons, cylinders
and other devices to produce a movement in one
place, using pressure at another place, and to
increase or decrease pressure.

Gyroscope

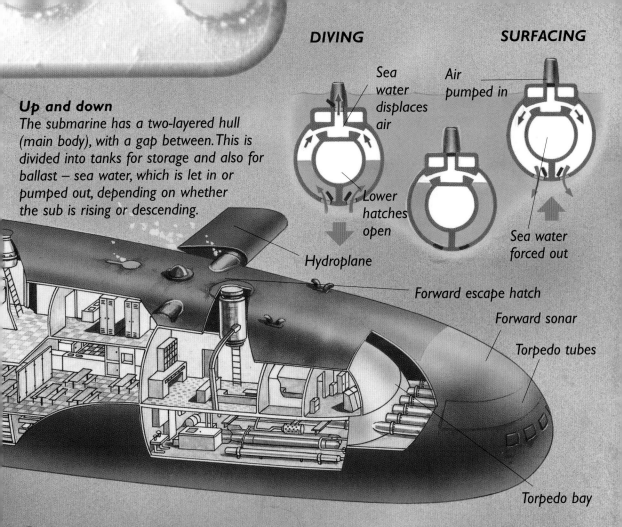

DIVING

Sea water displaces air

Lower hatches open

SURFACING

Air pumped in

Sea water forced out

Up and down

The submarine has a two-layered hull (main body), with a gap between. This is divided into tanks for storage and also for ballast – sea water, which is let in or pumped out, depending on whether the sub is rising or descending.

Hydroplane

Forward escape hatch

Forward sonar

Torpedo tubes

Torpedo bay

Gyroscope

Submarines use gyroscopes for navigation and to stay steady in rough seas and strong currents. The gyro has a wheel that spins quickly and stays steady.

Submarine hydraulics

A submarine has dozens of hydraulic devices, connected by pipes of pressurized oil. The hydroplanes at the front of the vessel and the rudders at the rear are tilted up and down by hydraulic pistons. Hydroplanes make the front angle upwards so the submarine is able to surface.

VIBRATIONS

Energy of vibrations

Sound waves are vibrations in a substance, rippling outwards from a source. The vibrations gradually fade as their energy spreads and weakens. Sounds pass through gases, liquids and solids. We usually hear sounds that travel through gases (air). Sounds move more rapidly, for longer distances, through liquids. They go even faster and farther in solids. Sound energy needs atoms for its passage, so it cannot travel through a vacuum such as space.

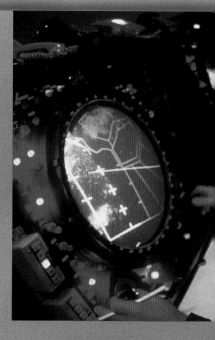

Sonar

Ships use sonar to detect objects in the water, including the seabed. Powerful pulses or 'pings' of sound from an emitter are reflected or bounced back as echoes. These are detected, analyzed by computer and displayed on a screen.

Radar

Radar is the radio-wave version of sonar (left). Radio waves are sent into the sky where objects such as planes, clouds and tall buildings reflect them back, for detection and analysis. Results are usually updated every few seconds and displayed on a screen. Radar is especially useful for air traffic control, to track aircraft around an airport, and to detect clouds for weather forecasting.

20.96′ E
48.18′ N

GPS satellite

Satellite navigation
Radio signals are sent to the surface of the Earth by 24 orbiting satellites. At any place on the planet, signals from at least three satellites can be detected and compared by a hand-held receiver, to fix a location within 10–50 m. The whole set-up is called the GPS, Global Positioning System, sometimes known as 'satellite navigation'.

Satellites orbit in six groups

Direction and ranging
In sonar, the direction from which echoes return shows the direction of the object. Also the speed of sound in water is known, so the time taken for a sound pulse to travel to the object and back again, shows the range – the distance to the object.

HEAT ENERGY

Getting bigger

The form of energy called heat is based on the movements of atoms and molecules in a substance. These do not stay still, even in a solid. They move or vibrate around a central area. In a very cold substance, these vibrations are small. As energy is supplied to the atoms and molecules, they move more, and faster. The substance gets hotter, and also larger, which is known as thermal expansion. If the supply of energy ceases, then as the heat energy is given off, the substance cools down and shrinks or contracts.

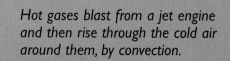

Hot gases blast from a jet engine and then rise through the cold air around them, by convection.

Seeking heat

Some types of missiles search out their target by sensing the heat energy that it gives off. Both jet and propeller planes have engines that leave an invisible trail of hot gases behind them as they fly. The missile's sensors 'scan' the sky and detect this heat by the rays it emits, which are called infra-red waves. The missile then locks onto the heat trail and follows it right up to the engine's exhaust.

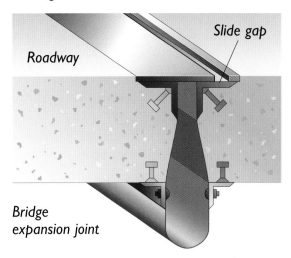

Roadway

Slide gap

Bridge expansion joint

Expansion problems

Many machines, engines and structures have metal parts, and most metals expand as they become warm. Hot weather can cause problems for metal bridges and railway lines, as they grow in length. So gaps or sliding joints are designed to allow for this.

How heat moves

Heat energy moves in three main ways. As atoms and molecules become warmer, they vibrate more, bump into atoms and molecules around them, and set them vibrating, too. Gradually the vibrations spread through a substance. This is thermal conduction.

Hot coffee conducts heat to cup

As a substance becomes hot and expands, its atoms and molecules move slightly farther apart. The substance becomes less dense. If it is a region of a liquid or gas, and can flow, it rises above its cooler, denser surroundings, carrying heat with it. This is convection. A third way in which heat moves is radiation, as infra-red rays (part of the EM spectrum of rays and waves). These can travel through space – it's how the Sun heats Earth.

LIGHT

Waves we can see

Light is one way in which energy moves from place to place. Light waves are similar in nature to radio waves, microwaves and X-rays. They are a form of energy called electromagnetic (EM) radiation. This consists of a combination of electricity and magnetism, becoming stronger in peaks, then weaker in troughs, in a wave-like fashion. Light and all other forms of EM waves travel at the same speed, which we usually call the speed of light. This is about 300,000 km/sec – a million times faster than sound waves.

Pieces of light

Swiss-American scientist Albert Einstein (1879–1955) is remembered mainly for his work on the theory of relativity. But before this, he also worked on light. At the time, light was regarded only as waves. Einstein went back to a much  older idea, that light might also be viewed as units or particles, called photons. In 1905 he explained how light can be converted into electricity.

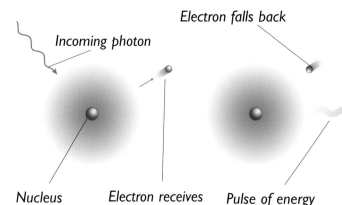

Incoming photon

Electron falls back

Nucleus of atom

Electron receives extra energy

Pulse of energy released

Waves and particles

Light can be viewed as tiny packets of energy called photons. When a photon hits a certain type of atom, it gives the atom extra energy, which can make one of the atom's electrons jump into a different position. Later, when the electron jumps back, the atom gives out a burst of energy. This may be as light, X-rays or radio waves.

Colours of light

Light waves have a range of lengths, although all are very short, with thousands of waves stretching only one millimetre. We see the longest light waves as the colour red, medium-length ones as green, and the shortest light waves as blue and violet. All of these different colours make up the visible spectrum of light — the colours of the rainbow.

Inventing light

Electricity can be changed into light by many devices. The most common is the light bulb. An early type of light bulb was developed in 1879 by American inventor and engineer, Thomas Edison (1847–1931). His team of workers tested more than 4000 substances that glowed white-hot when electricity passed through them. Edison also invented an early type of sound recorder-player, called the phonograph, and a kind of microphone.

RADIOACTIVITY

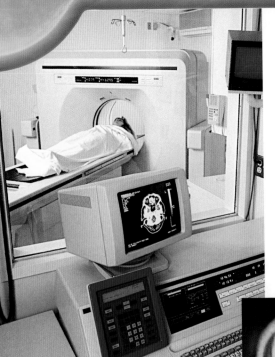

Radioactivity

Radioactivity is a particular type of energy that is given off, or radiated, by the nuclei (centres) of certain atoms. It may be very harmful to living things, including the human body. Radioactivity is produced by the breakdown, or decay, of nuclei, which are unbalanced or unstable for some reason. As the nuclei decay, they give off three possible kinds of radioactivity, called alpha, beta and gamma. Although radioactivity may be harmful, it can also be used to treat disease.

Seeing disease
Tiny, harmless amounts of radioactivity can help to pinpoint diseased parts. A biochemical substance that is taken up by a certain part of the body is made radioactive, and then put into the body, by injection or being eaten. A special radioactivity-sensing scanner or camera takes pictures of where the substance is concentrated. Unusual amounts or sites indicate problems such as tumours.

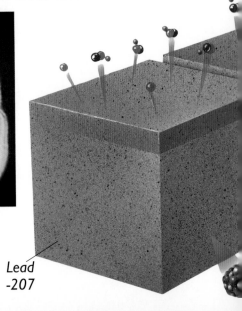

Lead
-207

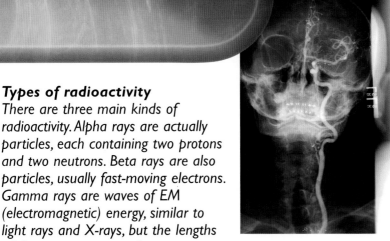

Types of radioactivity

There are three main kinds of radioactivity. Alpha rays are actually particles, each containing two protons and two neutrons. Beta rays are also particles, usually fast-moving electrons. Gamma rays are waves of EM (electromagnetic) energy, similar to light rays and X-rays, but the lengths of the waves are very short.

Radiotherapy

The harmful effects of radioactivity can be harnessed as radiotherapy. For example, in a brain tumour, cells multiply out of control. A small pellet of radioactive substance put into the site can send out enough radioactivity to damage the cells of the tumour around it, but not healthy tissues farther away.

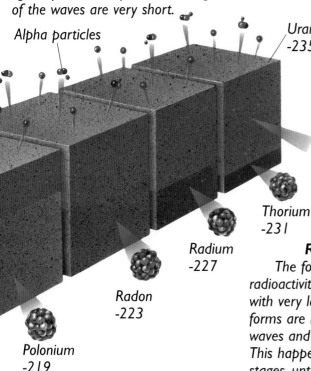

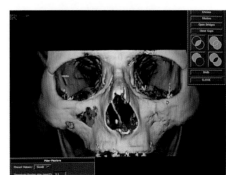

Alpha particles

Uranium -235

Thorium -231

Radium -227

Radon -223

Polonium -219

Radioactive decay

The form of a chemical element that gives off radioactivity is called its radio-isotope. For elements with very large nuclei, such as uranium and radium, all forms are radio-isotopes. As the nuclei decay, giving off waves and particles, they change into other elements. This happens at a constant rate, through various stages, until a stable end product is reached. Uranium-235 gradually decays into lead-207.

RADIO WAVES

Invisible power

Switch on a portable radio set anywhere in the world and you can tune into a programme. Radio waves are always all around us. They are a form of EM (electromagnetic) energy, similar in nature to light waves, and travelling at the same speed. Radio waves are invisible. They vary in length from several kilometres to about one metre. Radio waves are produced by a radio transmitter, when an electric current changes direction, or oscillates, very quickly. Natural objects such as lightning and stars also produce radio waves.

Receiving the Universe

Radio waves come from a variety of objects deep in space, such as stars, galaxies, quasars and the edges of black holes. The waves are very faint, so they are collected by huge antennae shaped like dishes or bowls. These are called radio-telescopes. Here on Earth, our own radio waves can be altered, or modulated, to carry information. The alterations may be in the heights of the waves (amplitude modulation, AM). Or they are in the number of waves per second (frequency modulation, FM).

Receiving radio

The shape of an antenna affects how it detects radio signals.

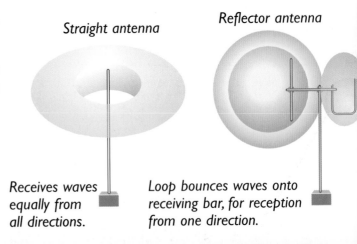

Straight antenna

Reflector antenna

Receives waves equally from all directions.

Loop bounces waves onto receiving bar, for reception from one direction.

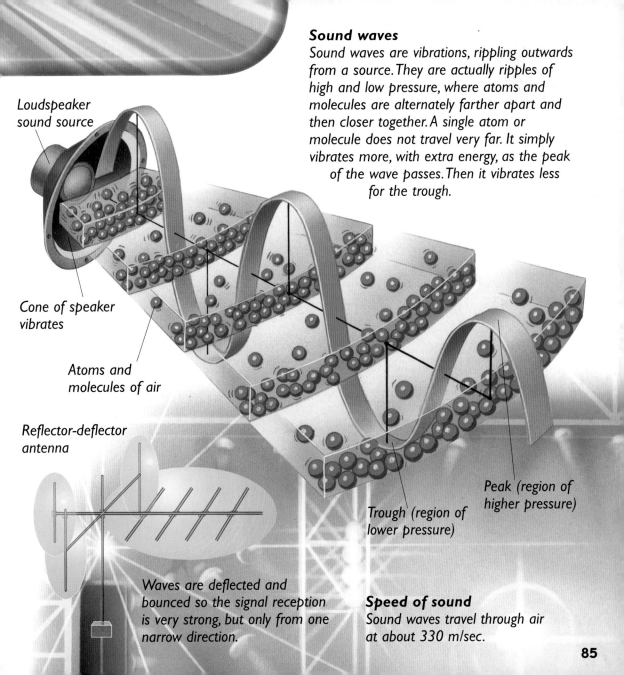

Sound waves

Sound waves are vibrations, rippling outwards from a source. They are actually ripples of high and low pressure, where atoms and molecules are alternately farther apart and then closer together. A single atom or molecule does not travel very far. It simply vibrates more, with extra energy, as the peak of the wave passes. Then it vibrates less for the trough.

Loudspeaker sound source

Cone of speaker vibrates

Atoms and molecules of air

Reflector-deflector antenna

Peak (region of higher pressure)

Trough (region of lower pressure)

Waves are deflected and bounced so the signal reception is very strong, but only from one narrow direction.

Speed of sound

Sound waves travel through air at about 330 m/sec.

X-RAYS

Very short waves

X-rays were discovered in 1895 by German physics professor Wilhelm Roentgen. He did not understand their nature, so he called them X-rays – 'X' for 'unknown'. They are now known to be similar in nature to radio waves and light rays – electromagnetic (EM) waves composed of ripples of electrical and magnetic energy. However the waves of X-rays are very short in length, much shorter than light waves. About 10 million X-rays in a row would only stretch one millimetre.

X-rated mystery

Wilhelm Roentgen (1845–1923) carried out experiments with a discharge tube. This passes high-voltage electricity through a vacuum or certain gases. He noticed that a nearby piece of card coated with a barium-containing chemical glowed when the tube was switched on. Roentgen guessed the tube gave off previously unknown waves, which for a time were called Roentgen rays, but we now know them as X-rays.

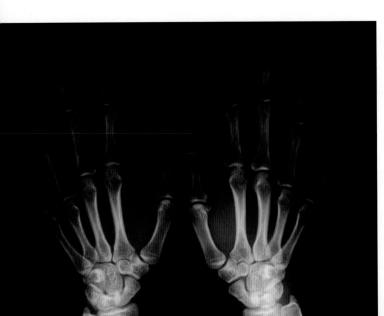

See-through rays

X-rays are powerful and penetrating, which means they pass straight through substances such as card, wood and the flesh of the body. They are stopped by harder, heavier, denser substances such as teeth, bone and lead.

How an x-ray machine works

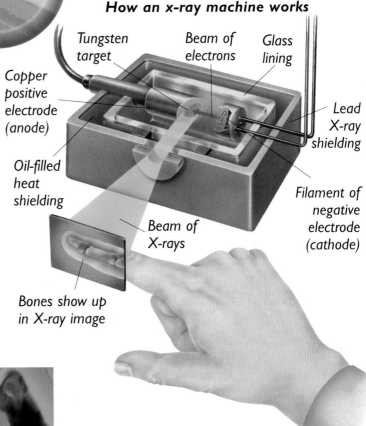

Tungsten target

Beam of electrons

Glass lining

Copper positive electrode (anode)

Lead X-ray shielding

Oil-filled heat shielding

Filament of negative electrode (cathode)

Beam of X-rays

Bones show up in X-ray image

Making X-rays

In one type of X-ray machine, electricity at 100,000 volts is passed between two electrodes. The electricity is in the usual form of electrons. They flow from the negative electrode, which is a very hot, glowing filament of wire, across a gap to the positive electrode, which is a massive copper block to absorb heat. The electrons hit a small 'target' of the metal tungsten, at such high speed that X-rays are given off.

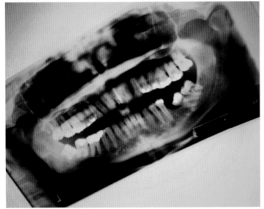

Teeth and jaw bones show clearly as white in this OPT dental X-ray.

Using X-rays

X-rays can be harmful to living things, including people. They cause sickness, burns and long-term problems such as cancers. However the X-rays used to show parts of the body, such as teeth and bones, are very weak. X-rays can also see inside cases and bags, outlining metals and similar substances.

SOLAR RADIATION

Lots of waves

Space is full of waves. Many objects in space give off vast quantities of energy in the form of electromagnetic or EM radiation. A gigantic source of such energy, which is relatively close to Earth, is the Sun. It sends out light, heat, ultra-violet and other electromagnetic waves, which radiate in all directions, and take about eight minutes to reach Earth. The waves are collectively known as solar radiation. Other objects in space send out powerful bursts of radio waves and gamma waves.

Background radiation

The COBE satellite (COsmic Background Explorer), launched in 1989, carried delicate sensors for microwaves. It discovered that microwaves are passing evenly in all directions through the Universe. This supports the idea that the Universe began in a gigantic explosion billions of years ago. The microwaves are often called the 'echoes' or 'afterglow' of the Big Bang.

Sensing waves

Hundreds of artificial or man-made satellites have been launched into space by rocket engines. The satellites detect various kinds of EM waves, such as light, infra-red, ultra-violet and microwaves.

Satellite photograph of volcanic mountains in Ecuador.

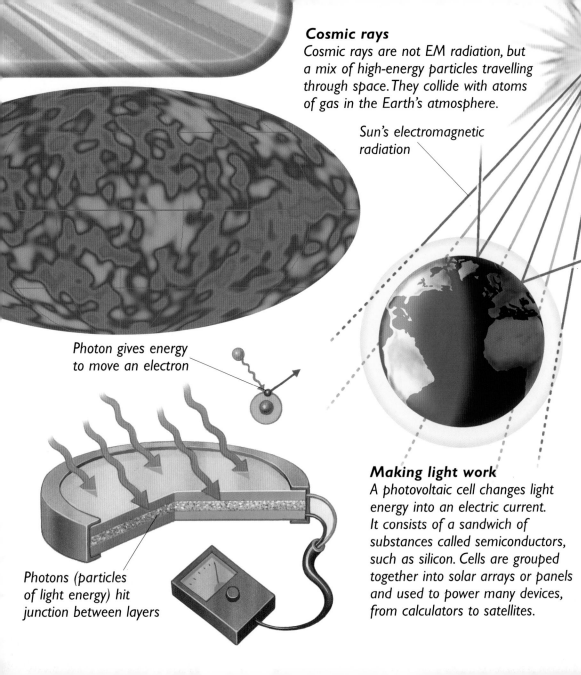

Cosmic rays

Cosmic rays are not EM radiation, but a mix of high-energy particles travelling through space. They collide with atoms of gas in the Earth's atmosphere.

Sun's electromagnetic radiation

Photon gives energy to move an electron

Making light work

A photovoltaic cell changes light energy into an electric current. It consists of a sandwich of substances called semiconductors, such as silicon. Cells are grouped together into solar arrays or panels and used to power many devices, from calculators to satellites.

Photons (particles of light energy) hit junction between layers

ELECTROMAGNETIC WAVES

The EM spectrum
Many kinds of rays and waves have the same basic form. They are ripples of electrical and magnetic energy, known as electromagnetic waves. They all travel at the same speed, which is named after one of the best-known types of EM waves, light. The speed of light is about 300,000 km/sec. Unlike sound waves, EM waves do not need atoms to travel, so they can pass through a vacuum.

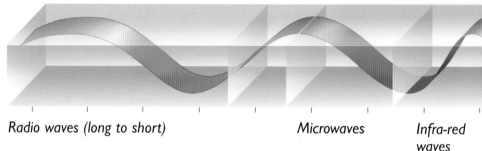

Radio waves (long to short)   Microwaves   Infra-red waves

Length and frequency
Along the EM spectrum, the waves gradually become shorter. In 'long wave' radio, they are many kilometres in length. Microwaves are generally from one metre to about one millimetre in length. Gamma rays have a wavelength of billionths of a millimetre. As wavelengths decrease, their frequency – the number of waves going past in one second – increases.

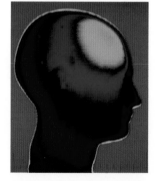

Infra-red
Heat energy is carried by infra-red waves. We feel the infra-red rays as warmth. Certain types of screen or camera films are sensitive, not to light rays, but to infra-red waves.

White light **Prism** **Spectrum of colours**

Visible light
Most camera films are sensitive to the visible light part of the EM spectrum.

Colours of light
We see each length of light wave as a certain colour. Longest are red, medium are green, and shortest are violet. All of these mixed form 'white' light.

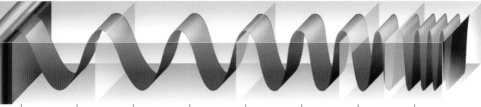

Visible light   Ultra-violet   X-rays   Gamma rays

Colours
When mixing light of different colours, the colours add together. Red, green and blue contain most of the wavelengths of light and mix to make white. The coloured substances called pigments, used in paints and dyes, take away light and mix to make black.

Primary colours of light

White — Red
Green — Blue

Primary colours of pigments

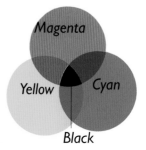

Magenta
Yellow — Cyan
Black

Fastest train

France's TGV (Train á Grand Vitesse, or high-speed train) *Atlantique* is the world's fastest train. It runs between Lille and Roissy. In 1990 it set a record speed on a national rail system of 515.3 km/h, although in passenger service TGVs normally cruise at 300 km/h.

Highest tower

At 553 m in height, the CN Tower in Toronto, Canada, is the highest tower in the world – almost twice the height of the Eiffel Tower. Helicopters were used to lift the topmost sections into position.

Longest bridge

Akashi Kaikyo Bridge reaches across 2 km of sea separating the two islands of Shikoku and Honshu, Japan. It is the longest suspension bridge in the world.

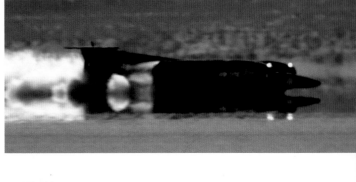

Supersonic flight
Only 16 Concordes were ever built. The world's only commercial supersonic airliner flew at 2300 km/h, crossing the Atlantic in under 3 hours. Concorde was taken out of service in 2003.

Speed of sound
Thrust SSC became the first vehicle to break the sound barrier on land. In 1997, Andy Green drove the British jet car at 1227.99 km/h across the flat sands of Black Rock Desert, Nevada, USA.

Titanic's voyage
Weighing 53,000 tonnes and measuring 269 m in length, *Titanic* was the biggest passenger ship of her day. On her first Atlantic voyage in 1912, she sank two hours after hitting an iceberg. It is thought that 1517 lives were lost and only 700 people survived.

93

AMAZING FACTS AND FIGURES

Michael Faraday

GREAT SCIENTISTS

Aristotle	384–322 BC	His ideas influenced most scientists until the 1700s
Galileo Galilei	1564–1642	Experimented with falling objects, discovered the pendulum, and used a telescope to study space
Robert Boyle	1627–91	Studied gases. Was the founder of modern chemistry
Michael Faraday	1791–1867	Pioneer of electricity
Marie Curie	1867–1934	Discovered radium and studied radioactivity
Albert Einstein	1879–1955	Changed the way people think about space and time

Petronas Towers

TALLEST BUILDINGS AND STRUCTURES

Building or structure	Date	Height
1 The CN Tower, Toronto, Canada	1976	555 m
2 Taipei 101, Taipei, Taiwan	2004	509 m
3 Petronas Towers, Kuala Lumpur, Malaysia	1998	452 m
4 Sears Tower, Chicago	1974	442 m
5 Jin Mao Building, Shanghai, China	1999	421 m
6 Two International Finance Centre, Hong Kong	2003	415 m
7 CITIC Plaza, Guangzhou, China	1996	391 m
8 Shun Hing Square, Shenzhen, China	1996	384 m
9 Empire State Building, New York	1931	381 m

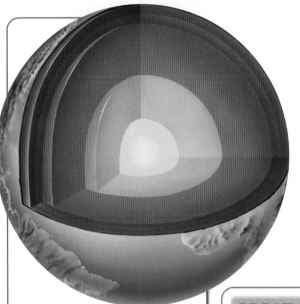

Chewing gum	1848
Potato crisp	1853
Tin opener	1860
Margarine	1869
Drinking straw	1888
Breakfast cereal	1892
Vacuum cleaner	1901
Frozen fish	1924
Electric toaster	1926
Contact lens	1948
Post-it note	1973
Clockwork radio	1991

DID YOU KNOW?

Although the Earth looks round, it has a bulge just south of the Equator. The centre of the Earth is about 6400 km from the surface and is so hot (over 4000°C) that the rocks there are molten, rather than solid.

GREAT LEAPS FORWARD

Electric telegraph	1837
Typewriter	1868
Telephone	1876
Voice radio	1906
Photocopier	1938
Transistor	1947
Microchip	1958
Laser	1960
Telecommunications satellite	1960
Computer mouse	1964

ANIMALS

From oceans and shores to deserts and mountains, this section is bursting with amazing facts about the world of animals.

How do bats 'see'?
What is the deadliest spider?
Why do whales migrate?

Read on to find the answers to these and many other fascinating questions.

ANIMALS EXPLAINED

SEA AND OCEAN

Far out at sea, there is nowhere to hide. The water stretches almost endlessly in every direction, and so danger can approach from every direction, too. However, animals of the open ocean still manage to carry out the essentials of life – finding their way, catching food and even building their own shelters.

SHORE

Where land meets sea is the world's most changeable habitat. Tides rise and fall, rain turns salty water into fresh, then disappears in drying winds and hot sun, until storm waves smash the shore to pieces. Sea creatures must be tough and nimble, or protected in shells, ready to eat anything the sea washes up for them.

RIVER AND LAKE

Water is vital for plant life, and where plants grow, animals are there to eat them. This happens along the banks of rivers and lakes, which also provide shelter for nests and families. The water currents also bring food for aquatic creatures. The river's links with the sea means that animals can migrate in various directions.

SWAMP

The world of marshes, swamps and other wetlands suits both land and water creatures. Many spend their early lives in the water, then come out onto land as adults, or even take to the air. Migrants arrive to take advantage of plentiful food in summer. They leave as the plants wither and pools freeze in winter.

RAINFOREST

No habitat is richer in wildlife than the tropical rainforest. Animals are active day and night, all through the year, as they find food, set up nests and other homes, or try to attract breeding partners. However, predators and other dangers lurk behind almost every leaf.

WOODLAND

In the woods, spring is a busy time. As the shoots and leaves appear, creatures shake off the winter, feed, and begin to raise their young. Birds and butterflies flit among the branches by day, while bats and owls take over at night. The old leaves on the woodland floor hide a miniature but fierce struggle for survival.

GRASSLAND

With few trees or rocks to use for shelter, animals of the grasslands have two main ways of survival. Some are large and fast to catch prey or escape predators. Others dig and burrow to make homes and shelters. Many grasslands suffer from droughts and wildfires.

DESERT

Even the world's driest places are home to plant and animal life. Creatures have many special features to cope with thorny plant food, the lack of water, scorching sun, shifting sands and hunters. Many of the smaller predators are poisonous. As prey is scarce, every catch is important.

TUNDRA

The tundra is the cold, windy, treeless land in the far north of the world, bordered by polar seas. The short summer sees light and warmth, when animals migrate from the south to feed on the plant growth. They soon return as the winter sets in. Creatures that stay must endure months of freezing temperatures.

MOUNTAIN

Moving around on mountains is difficult. Birds can soar above the crags, but land animals must cope with the steep, slippery slopes. Also, mountain weather can change in minutes, from warm, calm and sunny, to a howling gale and snowy blizzard.

Large front flippers for swimming

Flattened underside of shell (plastron)

Flippers and flukes
Dolphins live high-speed lives, swimming and leaping with great rapidity. They also sometimes move in mixed shoals with several other kinds, or species, of dolphin. The dolphin swims by swishing its tail flukes up and down. The front flippers, which are its 'arms', are mainly for steering at slow speed and are usually folded against the body when going fast.

Domed upper side of shell (carapace)

Safe in their shells
The turtle's strong shell is made of a bony inner layer covered by plates of tough horn on the outside. The skin is leathery and covered in hard scales. Courting turtles do a slow, ponderous 'dance' in the sea as they court and mate. Then the female swims hundreds of kilometres back to a beach, where she digs a hole in the sand to lay her eggs.

Tail flukes have pointed tips so water slips past them easily

Courtship in the water

Ocean creatures attract a mate at breeding time, just like animals on land. Sounds and scents travel much farther in the water than in air, and sounds go faster too, so many ocean-dwellers make use of these to draw the attention of a breeding partner. Whales, dolphins and porpoises, in particular, make a whole range of squeaks, clicks and grunts as they court. As they come closer to each other they use touch as well, stroking and caressing their partners.

Suitable sounds

The dolphin's courtship calls are different from the many other sounds it makes, which are used for finding food by echolocation, or for contacting other members of its group.

Courtship colours

Cuttlefish normally live alone but come together in small shoals to breed. Each uses colour and pattern to signal its readiness to mate as waves of black, yellow and brown pass rapidly along its body.

101

PROTECTION

Giant shoal
Fish such as herring have no obvious protection except for their darting speed — and being in a huge group. The colony moves together, twisting and turning almost as one. The effect is to make the shoal resemble a single massive animal, a 'super-organism' that could confuse or frighten off predators.

When the gannet comes near to the shoal, the flashes and glints from the herrings' shiny scales make it difficult to pick out one victim

Seen from above
Shoaling fish are more likely to be seen than lone fish by predators flying above the water's surface, such as gannets.

Nowhere to hide
The open ocean is a very exposed place. There are no rocks or seaweed for shelter or hiding. Many animals use camouflage or swimming skills to avoid being eaten. But some, like sea turtles and the nautilus, have protective shells. The nautilus is a type of animal called a mollusc, a cousin of the octopus and of the various shellfish on the shore such as mussels, clams and whelks. It builds its shell out of calcium and other minerals it takes from the sea water. The nautilus spends its day resting before hunting at night, grabbing on to its next meal with waving tentacles.

Jet propulsion

The nautilus swims by sucking water slowly into a chamber inside its body. Then it squirts the water out rapidly through a narrow exit. As the water jet squirts one way, the nautilus is pushed the other way. The nautilus also uses bubbles of gas to help it rise and sink.

Hunting in the dark

The nautilus is active at night. It hunts squid, fish and other prey using its huge eyes and sense of touch. It detects ripples made by moving animals and grabs victims with its numerous tentacles, passing meals to its mouth in the centre of the tentacle ring.

Fleshy cloak-like mantle covers much of body

Tentacles grab prey

Huge eyes for hunting by night

Animal's body is in last section of shell

Squid are molluscs like the nautilus but have shells inside the body

PREDATORS

Danger all around

Land animals face the threat of predators approaching mainly from the sides, or perhaps from above, in the form of an eagle. But in the sea, danger can appear from any direction – including from the dark depths below. One of the ocean's most fearsome hunters is the shark. It detects the blood or body fluids of an injured animal from many kilometres away, and moves in for the kill.

Shark's pectoral (side) fin is used for rising or descending

Fish such as the shark swish the tail from side to side to swim

Front flippers used for steering

The slowest hunter

Jellyfish can only swim slowly, as they squeeze or pulsate the main umbrella-shaped part of the body, the bell. Their long, trailing tentacles catch and sting many small creatures, such as fish and prawns.

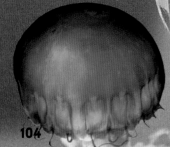

Natural defence

The humpback whale has few predators. At about 13 m in length and 25 tonnes in weight, its size prevents it from being attacked.

Whale's hairless skin slips easily through water

Parasite pests

Like land mammals, sea mammals such as whales suffer from blood-sucking parasites like whale lice. Other parasites, like barnacles, simply attach to and live on the whale, using it as a base but not sucking its blood.

No light to see by

On the bottom of the deep sea, there is almost no light at all. Some creatures here have huge eyes to peer into the gloom. Others find food mainly by smell and touch, and also by sensing weak pulses of electricity given off into the water by the active muscles of their prey.

MIGRATION

Yearly journey

Most great whales, such as the blue, fin, sei, grey and humpback, make yearly migrations. In spring they swim north or south, away from the tropics towards the colder waters near the poles. Here, their food such as fish and shrimp-like krill breed in incredible numbers, due to the rich nutrients stirred up by ocean currents. In autumn the well-fed whales swim back towards the warmer waters of the tropics for winter, where the females give birth to their young.

Sounding out the surroundings

Position of surroundings

Stun prey

Position of surroundings

Communication

Small whales, like beluga whales, can use sonar in several different ways. They can use it to communicate with other whales, or to sense the position of surrounding objects. Stronger sonar waves are used to stun enemies or prey.

Thick layer of fatty blubber under the skin keeps in whale's body heat

Courtship calls

In great whales such as the humpback, usually only the male sings at breeding time. He 'hangs' still in the water at a depth of 20–40 m and produces a series of moans, squeals and groans that last for up to 20 minutes. Then he sings the whole song again. The sounds travel for many kilometres through the sea.

Throat grooves

The humpback has grooves or pleats of skin on its throat. This allows the throat to expand like a balloon as the whale gulps in a huge mouthful of water, to filter small food items from it.

Calf (young whale) stays close to its mother

Natural noises

Whales may listen to natural underwater sounds, such as currents swirling around rocks, or through narrow channels, to help them navigate on their migration.

Tail flukes are mainly skin and muscle (they lack bones)

NESTING

Seabird colony

Gannets are among many seabirds that breed in huge groups or colonies. The colony, or gannetry is a noisy and crowded place. The birds swoop down in their hundreds, attacking and pecking any other animal that comes near. A gannetry may contain as many as 50,000 nests.

Parent gannets take food back to their young in the nest

Webbed feet for swimming

Untidy nests

The gannet's nest is on a ledge or steep slope, on an offshore islet well out of reach of land-based predators. It is also spaced apart from surrounding nests so neighbours are just out of pecking range. The nest is an untidy mound of seaweed and various bits of debris.

Processed food

Shore birds such as the gannet catch and swallow fish and other food, sometimes far out at sea. When they return to the nests, the food is already partly digested and soft. The parent bird regurgitates (brings up) this prepared meal for its nestlings.

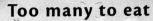

Too many to eat

One threat facing a baby animal is the predators who want to eat it. Along coasts and shores there are many hunters. One way of reducing the danger is to breed in a big colony, all at the same time. There are many parents to guard against enemies. There are so many youngsters that they cannot all be eaten. Predators are swamped with too much food and so many offspring survive.

Nesting alone

Coastal birds of prey such as sea eagles nest in single pairs. The eyrie (nest) is a large pile of twigs and sticks in a tree or on a steep crag. The female sits on the eggs to incubate them, with the male taking over for short periods while she catches fish.

Puffins breed in crowded colonies, with each pair of birds hatching a single chick

Oystercatcher prises open shellfish with its strong beak

LAND AND SEA

Taking the plunge

Most seas and oceans teem with fish, shellfish, worms and other creatures, which are a plentiful source of food. But there are also dangers such as sharks and poisonous jellyfish. So some animals have dual lives. They rest and breed on land, but hunt for food in the water, including otters, water shrews, seals, sea lions and crocodiles. The shores of lakes, rivers and seas are ideal places for this type of land-and-water lifestyle.

Wings for swimming

Penguins have strong wings but they cannot fly – at least, not in the air. However, they make flapping movements very similar to flying when underwater. The penguin holds its beak, head and neck out straight in front and folds its feet back, to make itself more streamlined for greater swimming speed.

Catching oysters

The oystercatcher feeds not only on oysters, but on mussels, clams, limpets, crabs, shrimps and worms, too. It has a chisel-like bill and strong neck muscles to stab and strike its food, carefully picking its spot to crack or lever open the shell.

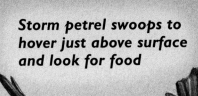

Storm petrel swoops to hover just above surface and look for food

Supreme swimmers

Grey seals look clumsy on land, as they wriggle up onto the rocks to rest. But when they dive into the water they swim with amazing speed and grace, swishing the rear end of the body and 'kicking' each rear flipper in turn. The front flippers are used for sudden stops and turns.

An oceanic life

Storm petrels only come onto land to breed. They spend the rest of their lives along coasts or far out at sea, feeding and sleeping on the wing or floating on the waves.

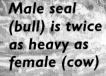

Male seal (bull) is twice as heavy as female (cow)

Seal's smooth, streamlined body slips easily through water

Fish hunters

Seals feed mainly on fish and the grey seal, which grows more than 2 m in length, needs about 10 kg each day. It mainly eats larger fish such as salmon, cod and whiting.

FEEDING AT THE SHORELINE

Making a meal of rubbish

The sea washes up a regular supply of old seaweed, dead fish and other bits and pieces of rotting plants and animals. This is all food for the scavengers of the shore, such as crabs. They sift through the mud, sand, pebbles and debris, and eat anything nutritious, helping to keep the coast clear of nature's leftovers.

Hard-cased crab

Shore crabs have shell-like body cases to protect them, not only against the beaks, teeth and suckers of predators, but also against coastal hazards such as crashing waves and rolling pebbles. If the crab's leg is trapped under a rock, it can detach itself without too much harm.

Many sets of mouthparts sort and filter food

Simple animals called sea squirts stick to rocks, taking in a continuous flow of water to sieve for plankton

First pair of limbs specialized as strong pincers

Slow starfish

The starfish is a slow but relentless predator. It wraps its arms around the shell of a victim such as a mussel, grips with its hundreds of sucker-tipped tube feet, and begins to pull hard. As some tube feet tire, others resume their grip, in relays. Finally the shellfish gapes open and the starfish turns its own stomach inside out to digest the exposed flesh.

A good grip

Many sea creatures, including starfish, limpets and octopuses, use suckers. The surrounding water makes a good seal and presses hard around the edge of each sucker, so that it is more effective than it would be in air.

Mouth in middle of underside of starfish

Jet propulsion

The scallop's two-part shell is not only for protection. The scallop flaps the two halves, or valves, together and swims jerkily over the seabed, propelled by jets of water.

113

LIVING IN A SHELL

Slippery skin

The butterfish is named after its slippery, slimy skin covered in small, flexible scales. This allows it to wriggle through seaweed, between boulders and even across rocks from one pool to another. It mainly eats small worms, shrimps and baby fish.

Distinctive row of about 12 black spots along each side of upper body

Scales are small, leathery and embedded in skin

Worm's home

The peacock worm makes its house from sand and mud glued with hardened mucus. The tentacles withdraw if danger threatens.

Beautiful plumes

The colourful 'feathers' of the peacock worm are actually frilly, antennae-like tentacles around its head. They are coated with sticky mucus that traps tiny floating pieces of food. The mucus slides slowly down into the worm's mouth, carrying its micro-meals with it.

Crabs and similar sea creatures have short feelers or antennae on their heads. These sense not only movements and currents in the water, but also blood from an injured or dying fish.

Shells – own and stolen

Shores and coasts are some of the most dangerous habitats. Giant waves crash down with a force of many tonnes, rolling boulders as big as houses or crumbling cliffs into rubble, as storms batter the land. This is why so many shore creatures have strong shells for protection. Many are also fixed in place so that the sea cannot sweep them away and smash them against the rocks.

Recycled shell

Unlike other hard-cased crabs, the hermit crab has a soft body. So it climbs inside the old shell of another creature, usually a whelk, and uses this as a second-hand, mobile home.

Antennae detect movements and waterborne scents

PARENTHOOD

The riverbank nursery

Many baby animals grow up along rivers and lakes – especially the young of waterbirds such as swans and grebes. The young birds or chicks stay in their nest at first, where they are warm and dry, and fed and protected by their parents. As the youngsters become bigger and stronger, they can their leave the nest for short periods. They learn to swim and dive in the river, and to cope with the waves and currents.

Male guarding the nest

The male swan, known as the cob, stays near to defend the nest and his family against marauding animals. If danger approaches, he spreads his wings, bends his neck, opens his beak, hisses loudly and pecks at enemies.

Safe cygnets

Baby swans are called cygnets. Two or three weeks after they hatch, they start to leave the nest for short trips. At first they ride on their mother's back among her feathers. Gradually they learn to swim and find their own food. The cygnets grow adult feathers and are ready to fly about eight weeks after hatching.

Wide bill

The swan's large, wide beak can pick up all kinds of food such as grass, leaves, reeds and other water plants, and also water creatures such as snails, insects and worms.

Salmon leaps out of water to catch flies for food

Female on the nest

A swan's nest is a large mound of reeds, sedges and similar water plants. The mother swan, called the pen, plucks feathers from her own body to make a lining that is soft and warm.

Paired for life

Many birds choose a different breeding partner each year, but the female and the male swan 'pair for life', and they raise about four chicks each year. Some seabirds also pair for life, like the huge albatross (above). Albatrosses breed much more slowly than swans. They only raise one chick every two years.

Sharing babycare

Horned grebes build a large nest of floating water weeds. The female and male take turns to sit on, or incubate, the eggs. Both parents also feed the chicks and carry them around on their backs.

Grebe's sharp beak catches small fish, frogs and similar creatures

Nest is anchored by plants growing up from below

Male grebe feeds while female sits on eggs

CARING FOR YOUNG

Together for a while

Among the many different kinds of animal parents, it is the mammals who care for their young most, and for the longest time. The mother feeds her babies on her milk, and in some types of mammal, the father also helps to protect his family. Harbour (common) seals sometimes swim from the sea up rivers into lakes to raise their young.

On guard

Each female harbour seal gives birth to a single pup. She feeds it on her milk and guards it closely for several weeks. Gradually, the pup learns to catch its own prey and becomes independent by about eight weeks after birth.

Seal mother comes onto land to rest and feed her pup

Thick layer of blubber (fat) under skin keeps in body heat

Learning to swim
The seal pup does not have to learn to swim. It can paddle and flap its flippers strongly almost from birth, by built-in behaviour or instinct.

Salmon leap to avoid being caught by otter

Otter twists and turns after fish, frogs and other prey

Learning to feed

Bear cubs learn from their mother about how to find food and stay safe. They sniff and examine many kinds of food, from berries and shoots to the honey in wild bees' nests. They soon learn what is good to eat. Freshly dead salmon in the river provide an unexpected meal, and the cub remembers the time and place so that it can return next year.

Tiny babies

Newborn bear cubs are tiny compared to their huge mother, weighing only 0.5 kg compared to her great bulk of 200 kg. They stay in the den at first, but start to venture out and explore as a family after a couple of months.

Fish is scooped out with paw or grabbed in mouth

Fish feast

Bears gather at rivers as salmon migrate in from the sea. The fish produce their spawn (eggs) and, exhausted, soon die – providing easy food for the waiting bears.

Food for winter

Brown bears usually sleep deeply in their dens in winter. They live off a thick, fatty, blubber-like layer just under their skin, which helps to keep them warm and provide survival energy during the long, cold season.

119

JOURNEYS

Short-distance journey

River dolphins (below) such as the Amazon river dolphin, make small and regular journeys along the rivers where they live. They use their long and flexible fish-like bodies to swim quickly after migrating fish and other sources of food, making clicking sounds and listening to the echoes to locate prey.

Up stream battle

On their migration up river, salmon swish their long, flexible bodies to swim against the current, leaping up rapids and waterfalls.

Sockeye salmon

Eggs in the bed

Most birds and mammals put their energy and resources into producing just a few offspring, and feeding and protecting these. But most fish, such as salmon, give no parental care. They put their resources into producing thousands of tiny eggs, and simply leave these to develop on their own. The female salmon releases her eggs, or spawn, and the male fertilizes them with his sperm, or milt. The eggs settle in the gravel of the stream or lake bed and begin their development.

Female North Pacific salmon lays eggs

Return to home

Fish such as sockeye salmon grow from tiny eggs in the fresh water of streams. After a few years feeding on worms, flies and other prey, they swim out to sea and become powerful predators there. Then they migrate back into fresh water, to the streams where they grew up, to produce their own eggs. It can take more than five years before a salmon returns to its home stream, finding its way by detecting the scent of the natural substances in the water.

Long-distance journey

Common eels hatch in the Sargasso Sea in the west Atlantic and drift to Europe with the ocean currents, developing as larvae. They grow up in freshwater rivers and lakes, and swim back to the Sargasso Sea to mate.

4 years

3 years

Sargasso Sea

1 year 2 years

Bendy eel
The eel's body is long and flexible, allowing it to creep under rocks or explore in mud to find food.

Male salmon provides sperm

MOVING THROUGH WATER

Slim, smooth and sleek

The water of lakes and rivers is much 'thicker' than air, and more difficult and tiring to move through. Creatures such as salmon, eels and other fish, and mammals such as otters and mink, can move quickly through water because they have a slim, streamlined shape. Fish wave their tails from side to side to propel themselves forwards. Otters kick with their feet, and the flaps of skin called webs between the toes make a larger area to push back against the water, and so thrust the otter forwards.

Eel has long dorsal fin on top of body and anal fin along bottom

Twist and turn

River otters swim at great speed, twisting around in a split second as they chase prey. The main forward force comes from pushing with its rear webbed feet. The front feet are held against the body except when moving slowly, when the otter paddles with all four feet.

Thick outer fur contains waterproof oils

Strong leg muscles kick rear webbed feet

All tail

The eel seems to be almost all tail. To swim forwards, it wriggles its body from side to side in waves that pass from front to back. It can do the same but with waves passing from rear to front to swim backwards. It also undulates along the lake bed like a snake.

Feeling the way

The otter uses its bushy whiskers to feel the way in muddy water, helping it to detect prey such as worms and shellfish. When swimming quickly, the otter stretches its head and neck out forwards to make its front end more pointed and streamlined.

Otter floats on its back as it rests or eats its meal

Dense underfur keeps otter warm

Fast water

Rainbow trout are fish of fast-flowing streams, where the water contains plenty of dissolved oxygen. Some kinds stay in fresh water all their lives. Steelhead rainbow trout migrate out to sea, like salmon, and then return to breed.

No need for speed

Hippos are large, powerful animals with few enemies. They eat plants, so have little need to move fast. A hippo is not at all streamlined, being wide with a huge, blunt head.

Muscular tail swishes from side to side to help otter swim

FLYING AWAY

Flying in formation
Geese often travel on long flights in a v-shaped formation. Each goose saves energy by obtaining some lifting force due to the air pushed back by the goose in front. The flock changes leader regularly to share the total effort.

Large red damselfly, like all damselflies, holds its wings together over its back when resting

A common goose
The greylag goose is the most common and widespread goose species across Europe and Asia. In some parts these geese are resident, staying all year. In other regions they are migratory, flying north for summer and south for winter.

Like all dragonflies, the emperor dragonfly holds its wings at its sides when at rest

Coot's large feet help it to swim and walk across water plants

Yearly journeys

Swamps, marshes, bogs and other
wetlands teem with life during the summer, when
plenty of sunlight encourages plant growth in the
warm water. However, during the winter the water
freezes and survival becomes much more hazardous.
Some larger animals, especially birds, breed in the
wetlands during summer but then migrate to more
suitable places to avoid the harsh cold season. They
return next spring to breed again.

Swallows on the wing

Many kinds of swallow
spend the winter far to
the south, in Southern
Africa. They fly more than
5000 km northwards to
Europe in spring, often to
the same nest site that
they used the year before.
Swallows feed and even
sleep on the wing. They
swoop up high to catch
flying insects.

**Dragonfly cannot migrate
long distances so
lifecycle is
adapted to
seasons**

Long-distance journey

Swallows, geese and other long-distance
bird travellers use various methods to
find their way. Many navigate by the Sun,
Moon, stars, landmarks, coastlines and
prevailing winds.
Some have a
built-in
compass,
probably
inside the
brain, to
sense the
direction of
the Earth's
natural magnetic field.

SIGHTS AND SOUNDS

Beak opens and closes in 'bill-snapping' action

Mating flight
Swallows swoop and twitter as part of their courtship, and even mate in mid-air.

Well-developed head crest in breeding season

Head looks up in 'sky-point' posture

Neck bent in 'bow' posture

Dance of the herons
Herons carry out a ritual 'dance' for their partners. This helps each bird to check that the other is fit and healthy, and a suitable mate for breeding.

Courtship colours

The heron's beak and legs become brighter in colour during the breeding season when it is time to mate. It also moults its old feathers and grows new, brighter-coloured ones as part of its breeding appearance.

Air display
The marsh harrier flies very high, then dives at speed and somersaults in mid-air to impress its mate in courtship flight.

Heron has long, spear-like beak to jab at food

Male harrier gives 'present' of food to female

Sights and sounds for partners

As the breeding season arrives, most animals form pairs, ready to mate. Two important ways of attracting a partner are with sights and sounds. Birds carry out a complex series of displays as they stand and adopt postures, and also jump, 'dance' and fly in special ways. These displays are designed to show off their colourful feathers and are accompanied by songs and calls, which add to the courtship effect.

Don't notice me

The male bittern's mating call is an extremely loud BOOM – almost like a cannon going off! However at other times the bittern is a very secretive bird, well camouflaged by its stripes and skygazing posture, among wetland reeds and rushes.

WATER BABIES

Webbed feet
The adult frog has large rear feet with flaps of skin, or webs, between the toes. It swims by kicking its webbed feet, which form a large surface area to push hard against the water.

Dragonfly eggs
Dragonflies spend the first part of their life in water. A female dragonfly dips the rear end of her body under the surface to lay her eggs on the stems of water plants.

Altering shape
Marshes and swamps, with their mixture of water and land, are ideal places for frogs, toads and other amphibians. When young frogs hatch, they do not resemble their parents. They spend the first few weeks as long-tailed, legless tadpoles that live in water. They gradually change shape, grow legs, lose their tails and move onto land as adults.

Front toes lack webs

Older tadpoles — one month

Dragonfly nymphs
The dragonfly's eggs hatch into young forms called nymphs. Like the tadpole, the nymph does not look much like its parent, lacking wings. But, like its parent, it is a fierce hunter of small prey.

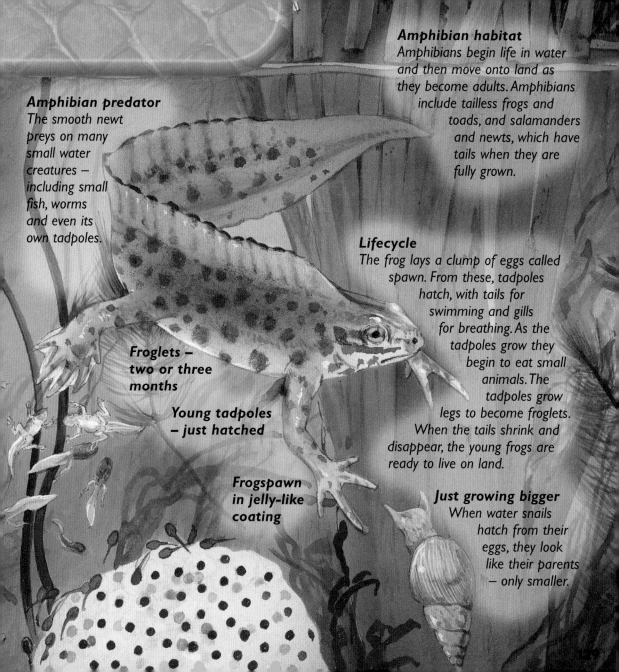

Amphibian predator
The smooth newt preys on many small water creatures – including small fish, worms and even its own tadpoles.

Amphibian habitat
Amphibians begin life in water and then move onto land as they become adults. Amphibians include tailless frogs and toads, and salamanders and newts, which have tails when they are fully grown.

Lifecycle
The frog lays a clump of eggs called spawn. From these, tadpoles hatch, with tails for swimming and gills for breathing. As the tadpoles grow they begin to eat small animals. The tadpoles grow legs to become froglets. When the tails shrink and disappear, the young frogs are ready to live on land.

**Froglets –
two or three
months**

**Young tadpoles
– just hatched**

**Frogspawn
in jelly-like
coating**

Just growing bigger
When water snails hatch from their eggs, they look like their parents – only smaller.

INSIDE SWAMPS

Useful fish
The mosquito fish preys on the water-dwelling larvae of mosquitoes that would otherwise change into adults and become pests.

Leech asleep
In dry conditions, the leech makes a case of slime or mucus around itself in the mud, and waits for its pond to fill again.

Very bendy, flexible body

More pointed front end has sucker and rasping, sharp-edged mouth

A sucker for blood
Swamps are home to various parasites — animals that live off others. Among such parasites are leeches. There are different types for each kind of host animal, such as the fish leech, the pond-snail leech, and the medicinal leech, which feeds on large mammals. To feed, the leech rasps a hole in the host's skin using its rounded mouth, edged with sharp, tooth-like spines. It sucks up the flowing blood and can swallow up to five times its own weight at one time.

Rear sucker at wider, back end of body

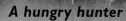

A hungry hunter
A pond turtle moves slowly, but it preys
on frogs, fish, water worms and snails. The
turtle hides in weeds or buries itself in
mud, and snaps at passing victims.

**Shell gives
protection and
camouflage**

**Sharp, horny
edging to jaws,
for slicing up prey**

**Head, legs
and tail can
be drawn
into shell**

Surviving
the drought

During a long, hot summer,
some wetlands may start to dry out.
The pools shrink and water creatures are
crowded into smaller areas. The heat also
drives oxygen from the water, so aquatic
animals that breathe underwater begin to
suffocate. Some can cope with the drought by
'sleeping'. They enter a period of inactivity called
aestivation, similar to hibernation. They burrow
into the mud for protection and stay there
until the autumn rains fill the pools again.

Two types of sleep
The European pond
turtle spends the cold
winter in hibernation,
inactive in the mud at
the bottom of the swamp.
It wakes up in spring to feed
and breed. But if the pools
dry out, it enters aestivation
and once again stays inactive
on the bottom of the swamp.

131

Mother and baby

Each baby gorilla sleeps with its mother in the tree nest she makes. Young gorillas stay with their mothers longer than almost any other animal, for three years or more, until the mother has her next baby. The mother gorilla grooms her offspring, removing dirt and pests from its fur and skin.

Evening tasks

As the gorilla troop settles for another night in the rainforest, most of the members climb into large trees for safety from poisonous snakes and spiders, and from predators such as leopards. Each gorilla pulls and bends branches over to make a nest platform, where it can rest and sleep. The largest members of the group, the fully-grown adult males or silverbacks, may be too heavy to sleep in trees. So they stay on the ground, at the bases of the trunks, helping to protect the troop above.

Well groomed

Adult members of the group groom each other's fur. This strengthens bonds between the gorillas in the troop.

Gorillas are active in the early morning, rest and socialize during the day, and feed in the evening

Sealed in a nest

The female red-billed hornbill rears her chicks in a nest inside a rainforest tree-hole. The male blocks up the entrance with mud and twigs, leaving only a tiny slit. The female cannot leave her prison-like home – and predators cannot enter. The male bird passes food through the slit to his partner.

Waking up

As the gorillas go to sleep, their tiny cousins, the bushbabies, are waking up. These nocturnal tree-dwellers leap through the branches with amazing speed and skill even on the darkest of nights.

Sleeping babies

Lesser bushbabies eat sap, bark, fruits, berries and small animals such as grubs. They sleep by day in a nest in a forked branch, well hidden among the leaves.

HOVERING FOR NECTAR

Cooling down

Hummingbirds save energy as they sleep by allowing their bodies to cool down by a few degrees. This is a kind of temporary night-time hibernation, called torpor. They warm up again at dawn, ready for action.

Beak and tongue

Each type of hummingbird has a particular shape of long, thin beak, designed to poke into certain kinds of flowers. The bird uses its long tongue to lick up and swallow the thick, sticky nectar.

Swapping places

By day in the rainforest, the air is busy with tiny, brightly coloured birds that dart about and hover in front of flowers. They are hummingbirds, and they probe with their long beaks into blooms to sip up the sugary fluid called nectar. As dusk falls, the hummingbirds find a sheltered place to roost for the night. Their place is taken by bats, which are nocturnal (night-active) but also hover in front of flowers to feed. Nectar-eating bats beat their wings fast to hover in front of flowers as they lick up the sweet liquid.

Torpid hummingbird is still and silent, but cannot race away from predators

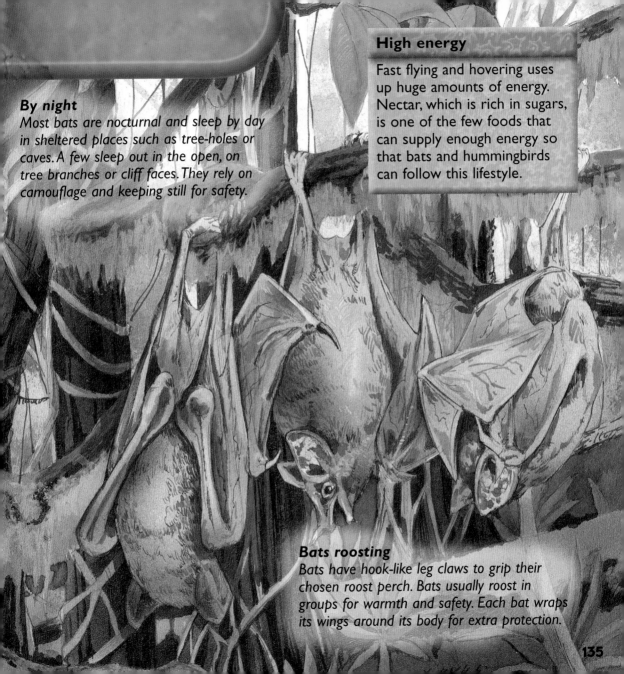

By night

Most bats are nocturnal and sleep by day in sheltered places such as tree-holes or caves. A few sleep out in the open, on tree branches or cliff faces. They rely on camouflage and keeping still for safety.

High energy

Fast flying and hovering uses up huge amounts of energy. Nectar, which is rich in sugars, is one of the few foods that can supply enough energy so that bats and hummingbirds can follow this lifestyle.

Bats roosting

Bats have hook-like leg claws to grip their chosen roost perch. Bats usually roost in groups for warmth and safety. Each bat wraps its wings around its body for extra protection.

TRACKING SCENTS

Busy woodpeckers

Golden-tailed woodpeckers usually live in female–male pairs. They make loud, harsh, laughter-like calls to each other, and at breeding time they chase each other up and down tree trunks.

Snake mates

Snakes cannot see or hear well, so they must rely on other senses, such as smell. When a female is ready to breed, she releases a scent trail. The male detects this and follows her. Most snakes lay eggs, although some give birth to young.

Scents and strokes

The rainforest is a crowded habitat where bushes, trees, leaves and creepers obscure the view. So at breeding time, many creatures use smells instead of sight displays to help them attract partners from far away. The smells waft through the jungle on the breeze and some creatures, such as certain male moths, can detect the scent from a female of their kind from over one kilometre away. When the pair come closer together, sight and then finally touch take over as they court and prepare to mate.

Female releases scent to attract male

Pond in a tree

Some tree frogs never go down to the ground, even to lay their eggs. Instead, they use tiny pools of water in large flowers and forked branches, high in trees. The frog whips up the water into a foam to help camouflage the tadpoles.

African rock python lurks, camouflaged against rocks and tree trunks

Smelling tongue

A snake tastes and smells with its tongue. It flicks out the tongue to gather airborne scents and senses these in a special chamber in the roof of its mouth.

Scents in the night

Many male moths have very large, feathery antennae (feelers). These do not sense general smells and odours. Rather, they are specialized to detect only one main scent – the substance called a pheromone, given off by the female at breeding time.

PROTECTING YOUNG

Baby on the back

Some active rainforest animals, such as monkeys and bushbabies, carry their young around with them. The mother bushbaby leaves her tiny, newborn offspring in a tree nest for the first few days. Then she carries it gently in her mouth to a place where she can feed, and puts the baby nearby on a twig. After a few weeks the youngster grows strong enough to cling to her fur. Gradually the young bushbaby learns to grasp twigs and climb by itself. It follows its mother at first, learning how she finds food and avoids falling.

Mother bushbaby pauses while feeding every now and then, to allow her baby to feed on her milk

Parked for the night

Bushbabies are named after their night-time calls, which sound like a human baby crying. When the mother puts her youngster on a branch, it stays still and quiet so that it is not noticed by predators. She feeds nearby, then collects the baby, moves to a new feeding place, and so on through the night.

Large, long, strong back legs for leaping

Bushy tail wraps around body when sleeping

In the pouch

Some animals carry their new babies in a special body part, the pocket-like marsupium or pouch. These animals are called marsupials and include kangaroos, wallabies, koalas, wombats and opossums. Marsupial babies are born tiny and almost helpless, eyes closed and without fur. All they can do is crawl to the pouch, attach to the mother's teat, and suckle milk. They stay in the pouch for many weeks, developing and growing stronger. Eventually they are able to leave the pouch for short periods, to learn how to feed and move about on their own. But if a threat appears, they quickly return to the safety of the pouch.

Clinging tail

Some marsupials, such as the possum (below), have grasping or prehensile tails. They can hang by the tail while feeding or watching for danger.

Balancing tail

The bushbaby leaps with its body held upright, using its long tail for balance, and clinging on with its long-fingered hands.

First journey

A new-born kangaroo is only 2 cm in length, but has to pull itself from the birth canal, up its mother's body to her pouch, to find a teat to attach to and suck.

DUSK ACTIVITY

The dusk change-over

As daylight fades in the woodland, there is a great change in animal activity. Diurnal (daytime) creatures such as warblers, hawks and butterflies settle down in a sheltered place among the leaves or roots, to roost or sleep. They are replaced by nocturnal animals such as owls, mice, bats and moths, which come out to look for food in the darkness. When light returns at dawn, the day and night shifts will change back again.

Birdsong
Warblers sing loudly at dusk and dawn. The sounds inform others that their territory is occupied.

Back to the chicks
Parent warblers return to sit on their nests, built on or near the ground.

A long day
Golden-winged warblers spend most of the day searching twigs, leaves and bark for caterpillars, beetles, spiders and other small items of food. As dusk approaches they find a place to hide and rest.

Thin beak probes for insects

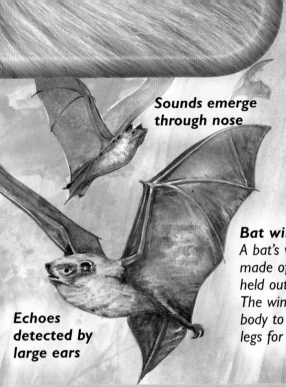

Sounds emerge through nose

Echoes detected by large ears

Low energy

As bats sleep by day, their internal body temperatures may fall by 5–10°C for a few hours to save energy. This is an everyday version of the much longer, deeper sleep they undergo in winter, called hibernation. At dusk, the body temperature rises and the bat wakes up, ready to feed on moths, gnats and other nocturnal flying insects.

Bat wings
A bat's wings are like its hands. They are made of very thin, stretchy, leathery skin held out by the long bones of the fingers. The wings stretch down the side of the body to the legs. Bats usually only use their legs for hanging.

Sounding out the surroundings

Sounds are useful in woods, where lines of sight are often obscured by leaves and branches. Bats make high-pitched squeaks and clicks as they fly, which bounce off nearby objects. The returning echoes allow the bat to detect the position of objects around it in great detail, even when it is in total darkness. This is called echolocation. Whales, dolphins and fish also use echolocation to help them navigate.

Bat roosts
Bats sleep in old woodpecker nests, or similar holes inside trees, or in crevices between rocks, and even in underground caves.

GROWING UP

Feeding new offspring

Many woodland creatures raise their young in safe, secure places such as nests in trees or burrows in the ground. The babies are too small to find their own food, so the parents feed them. Birds bring small, juicy items of food for their chicks. Their gaping mouths encourage the parents to feed them. Baby mammals such as badger cubs and deer fawns feed on milk from their mother.

Growing inside eggs

A baby bird inside its eggshell feeds on a yellow store of food called yolk. When it is time to hatch, the bird pecks through the shell.

Parents bring small caterpillars, grubs and other soft, juicy food

Chicks in the nest

Eastern bluebirds usually build their nest in an old woodpecker tree-hole or in the fork of a branch. The nest is shaped like a deep cup and made of grass and plant stems. The female incubates the eggs and the male brings food for her. Bluebird chicks are brown, and blend in well with the leaves and twigs so that the chicks are less likely to be noticed by predators.

Out of the burrow

When young badgers are about two or three months old they begin to come out of the burrow for short periods. They start to find their own food, and also roll and tumble together. This looks like playing, but the badgers are learning how to jump, pounce, run and carry out other actions important for their adult life.

In the burrow

Baby badgers spend the first two months safe in their deep burrow. Their underground home is called a sett. The mother leaves them in the sett while she goes to look for food.

Processed food

Like mammals, baby pigeons feed on mother's 'milk'. The pigeon can make a pale, cheesy substance in its crop (lower throat) which it regurgitates (brings up) as 'milk' for its nestlings.

Stag (male) and doe (female) deer begin to court

Claws are sharpened on tree trunk

Badger food
The mother badger goes off hunting at night. She catches many kinds of small animals such as mice, voles, lizards and birds.

Hidden fawn
The fawn stays perfectly still, hidden in the undergrowth, while its mother goes off to feed. The fawn's spots give camouflage among the leaves and stems. The mother deer returns to feed her fawn milk at regular intervals. Predators like wolves are more likely to spot the two together, rather than the fawn on its own, so she does not stay for a long time.

Fawn begins to move and feed after four to six weeks

143

Risky mating
Some male animals, including various spiders, run a great risk at breeding time – of being eaten by their partners. The female praying mantis is much larger than the male, and she may seize him even as he is trying to mate with her.

Egg parcel
Female spiders, such as the black widow, spin a strong case of silk thread, called a cocoon, to protect their eggs. The babies or spiderlings develop and hatch here but receive no further help from the parent.

Newly-hatched spiderling

Poison fangs

Recycling silk
Most spiders spin a new web each day or night since the old one is soon damaged by prey, big animals or heavy rain. The spider eats its old web to recycle its materials.

Sticky silk threads trap victim

Web among the leaves
Woodlands are ideal places for spiders that spin their webs among the twigs and then wait nearby. When a fly, moth or similar victim gets trapped in the web, its movements alert the spider. The spider then returns to bite the prey with its poisonous fangs.

Cocoon fixed securely to twig

Out on their own

Most young mammals and birds are cared for by their parents, but eventually they must leave their family and start life on their own. Insects, spiders and other similar creatures usually have no parental care after they hatch from their eggs. They must fend for themselves straight away. In the woodland, there are plenty of cracks and crevices among leaves, bark and roots where these small animals can hide. However danger lurks behind every leaf and twig, and most offspring are soon eaten.

Diadem spider builds large web in various shapes

Learning fast

Young mammals such as raccoons face many hazards. They may fall from a tree, or eat something which is harmful or poisonous. However, some foods, such as birds' eggs, are very nutritious and worth the risk of a daring climb. The youngster must learn quickly from its experiences to succeed in later life.

Deadly bite

The female black widow is one of the world's most dangerous spiders. She uses her venomous fangs to subdue prey, but she also bites larger animals or people in self-defence. Her poison is 15 times stronger than a rattlesnake's.

SURVIVAL

Notice me

Many hunted animals have fur that camouflages them in their surroundings. However, the skunk has a striking, easily recognizable pattern of bold black-and-white fur. The warning colours tell other animals that the skunk can spray a horrible-smelling fluid from its rear end to drive away attackers.

Long and flexible

The centipede's body is flat, long and flexible so that it can wriggle under bark, leaves and stones. It is one of the fastest of the tiny animals on the forest floor.

A fast hunter

The weasel is one of the smaller hunting mammals. But it is fast and ferocious, and tackles prey such as rabbits, which may be larger than itself. Its usual victims are mice, voles and young birds. The weasel's body is lithe, long and flexible, so that it can follow mice down into their burrows to catch them. Short legs allow the weasel to move and turn quickly inside burrows.

Sharp senses

Mice, voles and other small hunted mammals have very large ears and eyes, so they can hear and see well to detect danger. They also have very speedy reactions to leap away from predators and scurry away through the leaves. A mouse detects nearby movements as vibrations in the ground.

Down from the branches

Squirrels leap with great skill through the tree-tops. They come down to the woodland floor, especially in autumn, to feed on fallen nuts and berries. At all times they are at risk from predators such as martens, which are swift and agile.

Marten chases squirrel along a branch

Bushy tail helps squirrel to balance as it climbs

Centipede detects prey mainly by scent and touch, using its long antennae

Poison bite

The centipede hunts worms, snails, grubs and other woodland floor creatures. It has large, poisonous fangs that can give a deadly bite, and sensitive feelers (antennae).

A miniature jungle

The woodland floor is a tangle of fallen sticks and twigs, roots, bits of bark and old leaves, loose soil and pieces of flowers and fruits. For very small creatures such as woodlice, survival is just as difficult as for larger animals. Predators such as centipedes may be little but they are fierce. They hide in the leaf litter, wriggling and slipping through the undergrowth to seek out their prey.

147

SCAVENGERS

When death helps life

On the wide open grasslands, old or sick animals, or the leftovers from a lion or leopard kill, are soon spotted by hungry scavengers. Vultures, hyenas and jackals gather from far around, drawn by the sight and smell of the carcass. As they chew the skin, crunch the gristle, gnaw the bones and finish off the remains, they carry out the vital task of naturally recycling the dead body. Even the bones and teeth are picked over by ants, beetles and other tiny scavengers.

Chain reaction
Vultures circle in groups, evenly spaced apart. When one sees a likely meal it glides down. The others notice and follow, quickly drawing vultures from many kilometres away.

Junior members of hyena clan wait their turn

The strongest bite
The spotted hyena has an extremely strong jaw with powerful jaw muscles, and massive sharp-ridged cheek teeth. These work like shears to slice through skin, flesh and gristle. Hyenas can smell blood and meat from more than 10 km away.

Finding food

Lions usually make their own kills of fresh meat. But like other carnivores, they do not ignore an easier meal. A lion may chase a hyena, cheetah or leopard away from its kill and steal the carcass.

Ant bird perches on termite mound – a lookout place on the flat landscape

Keen eyes spot faraway victims

High view
The giraffe can see danger approaching, due to its very long neck and legs.

Long, probing neck
The vulture gets right inside the carcass with its long, flexible neck to peck up pieces of flesh with its sharp beak. The neck is mainly bare skin and lacks large feathers, which would become soaked with blood.

SUDDEN SPEED

Giant strides

Animals with long legs are able to run faster than short-legged ones, which is why so many grassland-dwellers have lengthy, slim limbs. In the giraffe's case, its extra-long legs help it to reach high into trees for leafy food.

Giraffes can reach more than 6 m high

Giraffes splay long legs to reach down and drink

Gazelles use tail flicks to warn each other of danger

Rapid runners

With few trees, bushes or rocks to get in the way, grasslands are home to some of the world's fastest land animals. The champion sprinter is the cheetah, accelerating to 100 km/h in under three seconds. However, top speed is not everything. Gazelles dart and zig-zag to dodge hunters such as the cheetah. If the gazelle can stay ahead for more than about one minute, the cheetah gives up. It runs out of breath and risks overheating after its massive muscle-powered effort. A cheetah will not attempt a chase if its prey is too far away.

Need for speed

Even the largest animals are capable of sudden bursts of speed. A rhino can charge faster than a human can sprint, at more than 40 km/h. It uses its great bulk and sharp nose-horn to fight off almost any predator.

Sharp horns and hooves used for self defence

Safety in numbers

Herbivores such as Thomson's gazelles, giraffes and zebras live in herds for safety. As they feed or rest, one or two are always looking up, listening or smelling the air for danger. A warning snort or stamp alerts the whole herd.

Struggle for survival

The hunt is part of the natural survival of the fittest. Gazelles that are old, sick or injured are more likely to be caught, keeping up the health and fitness of the main herd.

Ahead by a tail
The cheetah uses its tail as a rudder to turn at speed. Other grass land animals use their tails to whisk away flies and to signal their moods and intentions.

GRASSLAND SHELTER

Ant-birds feed on both ants and termites

Tunnels and ventilation holes allow cooling air to circulate around the nest

Big claws, long tongue
The aardvark rips open termite mounds and ant nests with the huge claws on its strong feet. It also uses these claws to dig its own home burrow, where it usually sleeps during the day. At night, it finds nests mainly by smell, but comes back to raid them in daylight when food is scarce. The aardvark licks up the tiny occupants inside the mound with its sticky tongue.

Sealed in a nest

In addition to termites and ants, bees and wasps also make homes for themselves and their young grubs (larvae). The grubs are sealed inside six-sided containers or cells. They are fed by the adults on mashed-up worms, insects and similar food.

Fennec fox eats mainly termites, so only needs small, weak teeth to chew soft flesh

Feeling and scratching

Meerkats are day-active animals and their main sense is sight. However they also have well-developed whiskers to help the meerkats to feel their way around their dark underground burrows. They also have strong claws to dig their burrows. Meerkats sit or stand upright on their mounds to get a better view of approaching danger.

Aardvark's burrow

Burrow system has many escape exits

Dug-out soil piled into lookout mound

Tunnels underground

Compared to a woodland with its tree-holes and roots, or a seashore with its weeds and boulders, there are few places to shelter on the grassland. Yet tiny, pale, soft-skinned insects called termites, which dry out and die quickly in the hot sun, survive here. They live inside huge mounds, which they build by chewing and shaping the soft earth into towering walls. Many other grassland creatures, from meerkats and aardvarks to mice, dig burrows and tunnels as homes in the soil.

TERRITORY

A valuable patch of grassland

In some kinds of zebras, the stallion (male) must keep a patch of grassland, called his territory, and chase rival stallions from it. Mares (females) only stay and breed with a stallion who owns a territory. Here they can graze more peacefully, since the stallion also helps to defend them and their foals (young) from predators.

Meerkat's warning yip means possible threat nearby

Ready to fight
Stallions communicate their readiness to fight by snorting, tossing their heads and stamping their hooves.

Kicking out
Rival stallions rear up and lash out at each other with their front hooves, or turn and kick with their back hooves. The winner takes over the territory and the harem (group) of females.

Sandy-coloured fur gives camouflage against dry soil and brown grass stems

Puzzling stripes
It is not clear why the zebra has distinctive black-and-white stripes. At dusk and dawn, when most big predators are on the hunt, the stripes may help to camouflage the zebra in the tall grass.

Waiting for a result
Zebra mares wait for the conflict between the stallions to end. A successful stallion may gather five or more females and keep his territory for more than five years.

Sharp teeth
Battling stallions may bite each other's necks as they fight for dominance of the harem.

15

GUARDING THE NEST

Protective father

Unlike most birds, it is the male ostrich who makes the nest and cares for the eggs. He does not need to keep them warm by incubating (sitting on) them, since the hot desert sun does the job. But if a hungry egg-stealer comes near he stands over the eggs, waves his wings and hisses loudly, ready to attack.

Partners aplenty

The male ostrich, unlike most birds, has not one but several female partners. The most senior female lays her eggs first, so they have the best chance of survival.

Large wing feathers make ostrich look big and fierce

Females lack large wing feathers

Huge toe claws slash at enemies

Need for speed

The ostrich cannot fly, but it is the fastest runner among the birds. Its long legs stride along at 70 km/h and so it easily escapes from most predators.

Shared nest

The male ostrich scrapes a hollow in the ground for up to five females to lay eggs. The nest may contain 15 or more eggs.

Nest defence

In harsh habitats such as deserts, food is scarce, and so creatures have to eat what they can, when they can. If a meat eater such as a jackal comes across a likely meal, perhaps an ostrich egg, it tries to take advantage. However, the ostrich is just as ready to put up a fierce defence. It flaps, pecks and kicks to scare the jackal away.

While the parent's away
Most parent birds cannot stay with their eggs all the time, since they must hunt. Reptile eggs are simply left by the female. Desert lizards, such as the gila monster, move in as soon as a nest is unguarded to steal the eggs.

Stone's throw
An ostrich egg has a very thick shell, which most birds cannot crack with their beaks. The Egyptian vulture uses a tool. It drops a stone onto the egg to break it.

Crouching low
The jackal's cowering posture communicates that it will probably not attack the nest.

The vulture can lick out the soft contents of the broken egg

TOUGH HERBIVORES

Prickly meals

Food is so scarce in the desert, that almost any plant is at great risk of being eaten. This is why so many desert plants, such as cacti and acacia, have thorns, spines and prickles to repel herbivores. Herbivores are equipped with tough mouths, hard lips and strong teeth to tackle their spiky food. Since trees are rare in the desert, many small animals dig burrows to find shade in the heat of the day.

Smaller herbivores
Prickles and spines do not deter small plant eaters such as the rainbow grasshopper. It crawls among the sharper parts of plants to eat the softer areas.

Egret pecks pests off oryx's skin

Egret warns oryx of approaching danger

Male's horns may be more than 100 cm in length

Fencing for females
In the breeding season, male oryx clash their long horns as though fencing with swords. They are battling for dominance so that they can mate with females in the group.

Egrets feed on insects disturbed by oryx

Versatile horns
The oryx uses its horns not only for battling rivals and in self-defence, but also to scratch in the desert soil. This exposes roots to eat, or makes a hollow where water may collect.

Finding food
Oryx rarely stay in one place. Plants are so few and far between in the desert that these antelopes are continually on the move, wandering many kilometres by night when it is cooler, to find fresh grazing.

Acacia thorns repel browsing animals

Balancing tail
The kangaroo rat's long tail helps it to balance as it leaps across the desert sand.

Rare rains form waterholes that attract many kinds of wildlife

Storing seeds
Kangaroo rats and similar small rodents collect seeds to store in their burrows.

MOVING IN SAND

Shifting sands

Desert sands and soils are loose, and slip as animals try to run over them. So desert creatures have different ways of moving. The desert sidewinding viper throws its body into a series of sideways loops. The sand skink wriggles like a fish and swims through the sand grains. The desert whiptail lizard has very long toes fringed by wide scales. These work like sandshoes to spread its weight so that it does not sink into the soft surface.

Looking for prey

The sidewinding viper half-buries itself in the sand at a suitable place to wait for passing victims such as gerbils, kangaroo rats or small lizards. In this position it is partly hidden from both prey and the heat of the sun. Like other vipers it has a poisonous bite.

Tough scales protect skink from sharp, rubbing sand particles

Swimming in sand

The sand skink can walk like a normal lizard using its four strong legs. But in very loose sand it folds its legs and feet against the sides of its body, and arches itself from side to side. It wriggles through the sand like a worm in mud.

Hard, pointed nose pushes through soil

Tracks in the sand

The sidewinding viper pushes its long body sideways against the sand, which makes it less likely to slide about on the grains. It leaves a series of J-shaped marks that look like tyre tracks.

No need for speed

The desert tortoise moves slowly and purposefully, and so slips less on loose sand. Its scaly skin and domed shell give excellent protection against sun and predators.

Toes cool in air flow

Any spot of shade

Lizards, insects and similar animals take advantage of any patch of shade, near a rock or small plant, where they can rest and keep cool.

Hard scales protect against touch of hot rocks and sand

Opposing front and rear legs held up at same time

The burning sand

Creatures out in the scorching sun can be burned by the hot surface of the sand. The desert whiptail lizard alternately lifts pairs of legs off the ground so its feet can cool in the air.

161

DANGEROUS DESERTS

The driest nursery

The desert is a dangerous place to live – and an even more dangerous place to raise offspring. Starvation, drought, predators and overheating are just a few of the risks facing young animals. This is why so many desert creatures show parental care, including mammals and birds, but also creatures like scorpions. They protect their young in a safe place such as under a rock, in a burrow, or in the scorpion's case on the mother's back, directly under her deadly tail sting.

Growing inside eggs

Many snakes lay their eggs and leave them to hatch alone. But the female python coils around her clutch of eggs and guards it until the babies emerge.

Fierce hunters

The desert sun-spider (solifuge) is not a true spider and lacks a poisonous bite. But its pincer-like fangs tackle small lizards, birds and desert rodents.

A venomous bite

All true spiders have eight legs and two large, poison-injecting fangs to subdue their prey. Many hide in holes during the day.

Pincer-like fangs

Cartwheels

To escape danger and reach safety, the sun-spider curls up its legs and rolls like a ball down the sand dune.

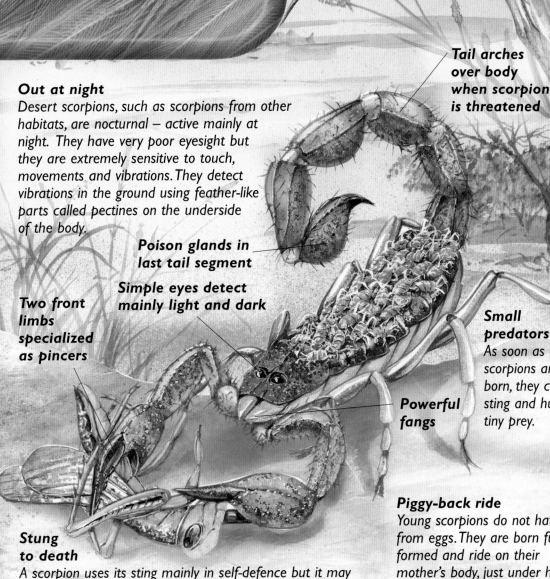

Tail arches over body when scorpion is threatened

Out at night
Desert scorpions, such as scorpions from other habitats, are nocturnal – active mainly at night. They have very poor eyesight but they are extremely sensitive to touch, movements and vibrations. They detect vibrations in the ground using feather-like parts called pectines on the underside of the body.

Poison glands in last tail segment

Simple eyes detect mainly light and dark

Two front limbs specialized as pincers

Small predators
As soon as scorpions are born, they can sting and hunt tiny prey.

Powerful fangs

Stung to death
A scorpion uses its sting mainly in self-defence but it may also jab prey to stop it struggling. It hunts insects such as grasshoppers, spiders, and small mammals and birds.

Piggy-back ride
Young scorpions do not hatch from eggs. They are born fully formed and ride on their mother's body, just under her poisonous sting. They leave her back after one or two weeks.

DAY OWLS

White for winter

Many creatures in cold northern lands, such as the ptarmigan and Arctic hare, have white fur or feathers. They blend in with ice and snow, so that they can hardly be seen. Merging with the surroundings is called camouflage.

Brown for summer

The ptarmigan's feathers change to brown in summer for better camouflage among grass stems and earth. In spring the Arctic hare's white winter fur falls out and brown summer fur grows back to replace it. This change is called moulting.

Owls out by day

Most owls hunt at night, under the cover of darkness. But nights in the flat, treeless tundra of the far north are too long, dark and cold for animals to be active, and so an owl would have nothing to catch. So the snowy owl hunts by day over the tundra. It glides silently and swoops down to grab victims in its talons (claws). It carries the prey to one of its perches and tears it up with its strong, hooked beak. At breeding time, it must catch more prey so that it can give some to its chicks in the nest.

Warm in the water

The polar bear may plunge into the icy water to catch seals. Its long fur coat and a thick layer of blubber (fat) under its skin keeps it warm.

Family meal

Snowy owls prey on lemmings, voles, baby hares and small birds. Their white plumage is camouflage against the snow-laden clouds, allowing them to dive down onto their victims more effectively.

Hunting in the dark

Most owls, such as the great horned owl, are active at night. They detect prey by sight with their huge eyes and amazing hearing.

Tail feathers fan out on landing, acting as a brake

Not quite white

The male snowy owl is mainly white with a few stripes. The female has more stripes.

Nesting in the open

Owl chicks are protected in their nest in the open by their mother.

LIFE ON THE TUNDRA

Heading north

The tundra has a short summer, when the snow melts and grasses, mosses and other plants grow. This sudden abundance of food attracts a variety of animals that migrate long distances from the south. Birds such as geese and terns can travel quickly by flight. Larger animals such as caribou walk, taking them several weeks.

The longest journey

Arctic terns make the longest migrations of any animal. As summer ends in the Arctic, they fly south more than 20,000 km to the Antarctic where summer is just beginning.

Grazing geese

Canada geese graze on grasses, mosses, and water plants in shallow, marshy pools.

Paired for breeding

The female and male geese stay together to raise their family. They may keep together as a pair for several years.

Tern hovers to spot food or danger

Risks of migration
Caribou, or reindeer, trek hundreds of kilometres north to feed on the tundra plants. When the cold and snow return, they will grow thicker fur and migrate south again, to spend winter in the shelter of the forests. Wolves follow their migration to pick off the old, weak and sick.

Unlike other deer, both male and female caribou have antlers

Finding food

Plants grow sparsely on the tundra. Caribou and musk oxen soon eat most of the lush vegetation in one area. They can either move on to find fresh grazing, or scrape with their hooves to reveal mosses, roots and lichens.

Two fur coats

Musk oxen stay out on the open tundra during the winter. They are kept warm by their thick fur. The outer coat has tough, strong hairs almost 100 cm in length. Beneath is the dense, softer fur of the undercoat.

COMMUNICATION

When asleep, fox uses bushy tail for extra warmth

Howls tell other wolf packs to keep away

Food from the freezer *Due to its thick fur, the Arctic fox is one of the few animals that can live out on the tundra all year round. It often scavenges on the bodies of dead animals.*

Tail held up, growl and ears pricked show dominance

Crouching, lowered tail, whimper and flattened ears show submission

Leader of the pack

Wolves live in groups called packs. They hunt on their own for small prey, such as lemmings and mice. The pack works together to catch large animals such as caribou and musk oxen. Members of the pack also help each other to stay safe, produce young and keep on the move. One male and one female wolf are the dominant pair or leaders of the pack. They communicate with others by body postures – using their faces, ears, legs and tails, and by sounds such as snarls and yelps.

Almost a fight
Sometimes a younger wolf challenges one of the pack leaders with bared teeth and snarls. But it's mainly a show of strength. The wolves rarely fight. If they did, they could be wounded and soon die on the cold tundra. Many animals put on shows like this called ritual displays, but rarely get into a real battle.

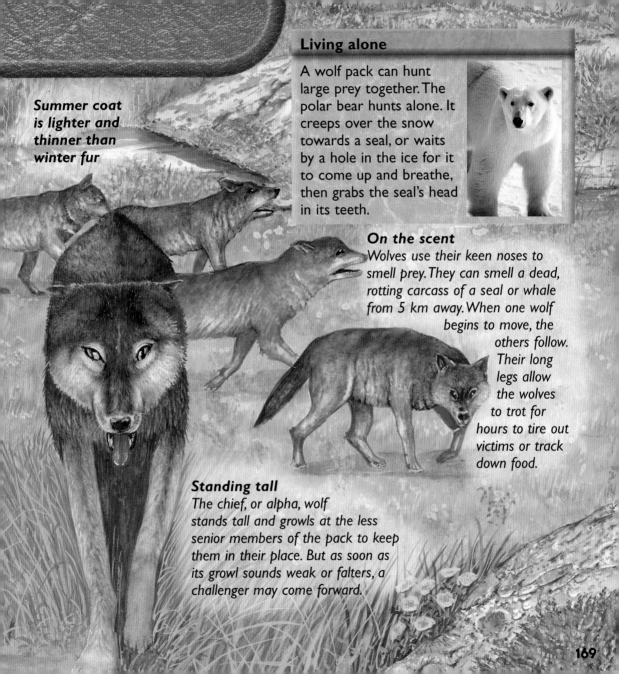

Summer coat is lighter and thinner than winter fur

Living alone

A wolf pack can hunt large prey together. The polar bear hunts alone. It creeps over the snow towards a seal, or waits by a hole in the ice for it to come up and breathe, then grabs the seal's head in its teeth.

On the scent

Wolves use their keen noses to smell prey. They can smell a dead, rotting carcass of a seal or whale from 5 km away. When one wolf begins to move, the others follow. Their long legs allow the wolves to trot for hours to tire out victims or track down food.

Standing tall

The chief, or alpha, wolf stands tall and growls at the less senior members of the pack to keep them in their place. But as soon as its growl sounds weak or falters, a challenger may come forward.

FEEDING

Active by day
Wolves and geese are diurnal, meaning they are active mainly during daylight, although hungry wolves may become nocturnal and hunt at night.

Wolf is bitten by mosquitoes and scratches its bites

Second thoughts
A wolf on its own may not risk trying to attack a goose or steal its eggs or chicks. The geese gather round to flap and peck at the intruder The wolf's lowered tail shows it may soon retreat.

Parasitic mites live in goose feathers

Canada goose stands its ground against threat of wolf

Active by night
Lemmings are nocturnal, meaning they are active mainly at night. They come from their burrows at dusk. They feel their way in the dark, and inside their tunnels, using the long hairs on their noses, called whiskers. Small ears, blunt nose and rounded shape prevent heat loss.

Busy eaters
Lemmings eat all kinds of plant food such as leaves, stems, and even hard seeds and roots. They gnaw with their long, sharp front incisor teeth, which, like those of many other rodents, keep growing, so they never wear down.

Safe by day

Lemmings sleep during the day in tunnels that they dig in the soil. They also flee there if threatened by a predator such as an Arctic fox or snowy owl — or by gnats, mosquitoes or other parasites.

Parasite pests

Apart from mosquitoes, several other kinds of small creatures are blood-sucking parasites. They include gnats, which are flies, and mites (right), tiny cousins of spiders, also with eight legs.

Tiny blood-suckers

Some animals who feed on other creatures are large and powerful, such as wolves. Others are tiny, like the mosquito. This small fly is not a hunter, but a parasite. It feeds by taking nourishment from another animal, the host, without killing it. Mosquitoes bite animals and suck their blood. Their hosts vary from lemmings and voles to huge caribou and even birds such as geese. The swampy bogs of the tundra are ideal breeding places for mosquitoes, whose larvae (grub-like young) live in water.

Sharp needle

A mosquito has a mouth shaped like a hollow needle, to pierce the host's skin and suck up its blood. It finds the thinnest area of skin to pierce.

171

FLIGHT

Flying high

Flight is the fastest way for animals to move about, especially over the rocks, cliffs, crags and steep slopes of the mountains. Birds can rise to great heights to look for food along the mountain range. They can also fly quickly down to the more sheltered foothills during storms or in winter to avoid the worst weather.

Primary feathers

Secondary feathers

Types of wing feathers

The large primary feathers at the end of a bird's wing are fanned and twisted for delicate control. The secondary feathers nearer the body are curved to produce an upwards force or lift (just like the wing of a plane).

Control in the air

The eagle uses its wings and tail to control its speed and direction. As the wind whistles past and buffets the bird around, the eagle continuously tilts its tail from side to side to keep its flight steady. The tail feathers fan out to slow the speed of the eagle's flight.

Wings for soaring

As wind blows against mountain slopes, it gets pushed upwards, creating rising columns of air. Birds such as eagles, condors and vultures glide round and round in these to gain height without even having to flap their wings.

Contour feathers cover body

Useful feathers
Feathers not only form flying and control surfaces, but give a smooth outline to the bird's body to improve streamlining. They also provide patterns and colours. The golden eagle is well camouflaged against the brown mountain rocks.

Smooth leading edge to wing

Highest nests
Some birds nest so high in the mountains, their chicks are safe from almost any predator. The alpine chough breeds at an altitude of more than 4000 m.

Killing claws
The eagle's long, strong toes are as big as your fingers and tipped with very hard, sharp claws called talons. These are for grabbing prey such as voles, rabbits, hares and even baby deer.

Feet and toes are protected by scales

173

COLOURS AND PATTERNS

Butterfly of the mountains

The apollo butterfly is found in mountains across Europe and Asia. It basks on a rock in the morning sunshine to warm up after the chilly night, then flies to look for flowers, where it feeds on their sweet nectar. Its wings need to flap strongly to cope with the mountain winds.

Female

Male

Front wing partly overlaps rear wing

Antennae

Butterfly wings

Most insects, including butterflies, have four wings (except flies, which have two). The two overlapping wings on each side flap up and down as one. The wings are covered with tiny scales of different colours, making the bright patterns.

Scents in the night

Butterflies, like many other animals, use smells as well as sights to attract a mate. The female produces an invisible scent called a pheromone, which wafts through the air. The male detects the scent with his long, club-tipped antennae (feelers).

Bright hues send important messages

Colours and patterns are very important as they convey messages to others. This is especially important on mountains, where the air is clear and the views wide open. Many bright colours are designed to attract mates at breeding time. As the apollo butterfly flits across the slopes in the summer sunshine, its wing patterns flash on and off like glowing lights to attract a partner. Other colours are designed to warn predators, to stay away.

Courtship calls

Female crickets make use of their long antennae to hear mating calls at breeding time. The male cricket chirps loudly by rubbing the veins on his front wings together to gain the attention of the female.

How butterflies breed

After courtship and mating, a female butterfly, such as the apollo, lays her eggs on the plant that caterpillars eat when they hatch out. This is called their 'food plant'. The caterpillars (larvae) busily eat and grow, shedding their skins about five times. Then they change into inactive, hard-cased chrysalises (pupae). After a few weeks the chrysalis case splits open and the adult butterfly crawls out.

Warning colours

The caterpillars of butterflies and moths move slowly and cannot run away from danger. So many are brightly coloured as a warning to predators that they have foul tasting flesh or body fluids. Predators soon learn to leave them alone.

Apollo caterpillar feeds mainly on the mountain stonecrops – its 'food plant'

HIBERNATION

Asleep for the winter

Winters are particularly long and cold on mountains, where snow and ice cover the slopes. Many creatures hide away during this time, in crevices and caves, or in burrows they dig for themselves. Warm-blooded mammals enter a deep sleep called hibernation. Cold-blooded creatures are simply too cold to move. As the spring warmth increases they wake up and are soon ready to feed and breed.

Communal den

Garter snakes spend the winter inactive in a sheltered hole where the frost and ice cannot reach. A hole is often used by several snakes, year after year. When the snakes stir from their torpor, they may mate in the den.

Underground village

Marmots spend the winter huddled together in their sleeping chamber. To save energy, their body temperatures drop from about 40°C to only 6°C.

Furry marmots

Mountain mammals such as marmots have thick fur to keep out the cold, strong winds. The fur grows even longer and thicker in winter for extra warmth.

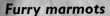

Food for winter

Like many animals that endure cold winters, the mountain beaver prepares by gnawing twigs and bushes, and storing the pieces inside its burrow under a large tree. This store of plant material should provide enough food to last the beaver through the winter.

Spring clean

When marmots wake in spring, they groom their fur so that it stays in good condition to keep them warm. Each marmot combs its fur thoroughly with its claws and teeth.

Marmot stands on hind legs to look for danger

Fur covers most of body and legs to keep in heat

COMPETITION

Battling for mates

In herd animals such as bighorn sheep, the breeding season is a period of fierce battles. The males head-butt each other to show who is strongest and most healthy. The females mate with the winners, so that their offspring are more likely to be strong and healthy. The mountains echo with the crashes and clatters of the males, or rams, as they bash their foreheads and horns together. The females and young keep their distance from the fighting and graze quietly.

Big horns
The bigger a male's horns, the more dominant or senior he is likely to be. Females and younger males have much smaller horns.

Strong skull and neck bones absorb jolts

Male rears up on back legs and lunges forward to butt

Strong neck and shoulder muscles increase butting force

Fight to the death
Usually one male bighorn is more powerful that its rival, and the contest is soon over. However, if two males are more evenly matched, they may head-butt each other for hours. Sometimes they become so dazed that they are knocked out, and one may become so injured that it dies.

Old enough to fight

Young male bighorns do not mature until they are seven or eight years old. Young females are mature at four years old.

The rutting season

Various kinds of sheep, goat, deer and antelope have battles between rival males at mating time. This is called the rutting period. In animals with branched antlers, such as bull elk (above), the antlers may become locked together and then both contestants die.

Strong legs and feet for leaping up crags and over boulders

Gripping hooves

Mountain hoofed animals such as bighorns have strong hooves with wide, roughened bases. These help to grip the rocks, especially when they are icy and slippery in winter.

Living alone

In some herd animals such as sheep and deer, the males live on the fringes of the group. In elephants, older males usually live alone and only meet the females briefly at mating time.

AMAZING FACTS AND FIGURES

Fantastic frog
A frog jumps by lifting its front legs off the ground and pushing off with its strong back legs. Almost any frog can leap 20 times its own length. The record jump is 10.3 m by a South African sharp-nosed frog.

House spider
The house spider can run at nearly 2 km/h. Relative to its size, that is like a human sprinter running 800 m in 10 seconds – much faster than an Olympic athlete.

Kodiak bear
The largest bears in the world are the polar bear and the brown Kodiak bear (right) of Kodiak Island off Alaska. These huge North American bears can stand 3 m tall on their hind legs and weigh about 750 kg.

Intelligent birds
'Bird-brains' are actually intelligent. Ravens and pigeons can work out simple counting sums. Parrots (right) and mynahs can mimic human speech, and some parrots can name and count objects.

Sperm whale
The sperm whale is the biggest toothed whale, measuring up to 18 m in length. It also dives to great depths, plunging to 3000 m to hunt for the giant squid.

Galapagos tortoise
At 1.35 m in length, the largest tortiose in the world is the Galapagos tortoise. They can live to a great age – 150 years or more.

AMAZING FACTS AND FIGURES

LONGEST, BIGGEST, DEEPEST

Longest worm	North sea bootlace worm	body length – 55 m
Biggest spider	Bird-eating spider	leg span – 28 cm
Biggest sea snail	Horse conch	shell length – 60 cm
Biggest starfish	Midgardia xandaros	body diameter – 1.38 m
Biggest jellyfish	Arctic giant jellyfish	body diameter – 2.28 m
		tentacle length – 36.5 m
Deepest-living sponge	Hexactinellida (class)	depth found – 8500 m

TOP PREDATORS IN THE SEA AND ON LAND

Killer whale:	Great white shark:	Elephant seal:	Estuarine crocodile:	Steller's sea lion:
9 m/9000 kg	4.5 m/3300 kg	5 m/2300 kg	7 m/450 kg	3.3 m/1000 kg

Kodiak bear:	Polar bear:	Grizzly bear:	Siberian tiger:	Lion:
3 m/750 kg	2.6 m/900 kg	2.5 m/400 kg	3.2 m/300 kg	3 m/250 kg

BIGGEST ANIMAL GROUPS (Number of Species)

Insects: more than one million	Plants: 375,000	Arachnids: 110,000 (spiders and relatives)	Roundworms: 100,000 (estimated)	Molluscs: 50,000

Fish: 27,000	Crustaceans: 26,000	Birds: 9000	Reptiles: 5000	Mammals: 4500

LARGEST WHALES

1	Blue whale	33.5 m
2	Fin whale	25 m
3	Sei whale, humpback whale	19 m
4	Sperm whale	18.5 m

Blue whale

HISTORY

From ancient Egypt and Greece to the Age of Empires and the modern world, this section is bursting with amazing facts about history.

How did the Egyptians build pyramids?
When were the first Olympic Games?
Who fought in the American Civil War?

Read on to find the answers to these and many other fascinating questions.

HISTORY EXPLAINED

ANCIENT EGYPT 3000-30 BC

Civilization, based on writing and city life, began in the great river valleys of Egypt, Iraq, India and China. Created around 3000 BC, Egyptian civilization lasted for 3000 years, surviving long periods of disorder, until it became part of the Roman Empire on the death of Cleopatra.

ANCIENT GREECE 2000-150 BC

The 300 warring city states of the Greek world destroyed themselves in the end. However, even their conquerors respected their legacy of medicine, drama, architecture, mathematics, the writing of history and study of politics. Our own alphabet came from ancient Greece.

THE ROMAN EMPIRE 27 BC-AD 476

Roman civilization was practical, a world of order shown through good roads, bridges, laws, sanitation and great military power. Even after the last emperor was deposed in 476, the legacy of Roman achievements remained an ideal that Europeans aimed to recreate.

AGE OF INVASIONS 800-1200

After 800, a new Christian empire took hold in Europe – modelled on the successes of the Roman Empire. During this time Christianity spread west to reclaim Spain and Portugal from Islam, and east to save Hungary, Poland and Scandinavia from paganism.

AGE OF FAITHS 1200-1600

Politics and religion remained inseparable. Christian Europe faced unrest as Catholics fought Protestants and it was threatened by Islam spreading to the east. Meanwhile in India, the Mughal emperor Akbar tried to rule Muslims and Hindus in harmony.

AGE OF MONARCHS 1500–1700

Gunpowder gave rulers the power to crush uprisings. Powerful kings and queens ruled in Spain, France, England and Russia. Further east, the Ming, Ottomans and Mughals ruled empires of even greater splendour with power unchallenged by Parliament or the Pope.

A WIDENING WORLD 1492–1866

Attempting to find a new route to China, Columbus arrived instead in America. Oceans became bridges between continents. The laying of the first Atlantic telegraph cable in 1866 made it possible to communicate with America in seconds.

AGE OF STEAM & IRON 1800–1900

Railways could run seven times as fast as stage coaches, distributing the cloth and other goods produced in factories. Rails, bridges and boats brought people to new lands like the prairies in the US, and kept them in touch through cheap postage and daily newspapers.

AGE OF EMPIRES 1763–1914

1763 saw Britain dominant in Canada and India. By 1914 its empire was the largest the world had ever seen. Africa, the Caribbean and most of Asia were controlled by rival empires, creating a way forward for trade, migration, missionary work and the spread of technology.

ONE WORLD 1900–TODAY

World wars destroyed empires, and new technologies created a communications revolution. Entering the third millennium, the urban lifestyles and the highly developed civilizations that began in the cities of the ancient world have now been adopted worldwide.

CONSTRUCTION

Construction for kings

The pyramids of Egypt were built as tombs for pharaohs (kings) between 2700 BC and 1750 BC. Egypt's fertile soil produced a food surplus, which enabled thousands of men to leave farming and work on huge building projects. Khufu's Great Pyramid is probably the largest free-standing single building ever constructed. Its base covers an area equal to six football pitches and is a true square to within 2 cm. Some of the building stone was cut from distant quarries and floated down the river Nile by raft.

Handmade bricks

Smaller pyramids were often made of mud bricks. These were shaped cheaply and quickly in simple wooden moulds and then left to harden in the sun. Mud bricks were also used to build houses.

Egyptian engineers only had the muscle power of men to help them create buildings. Modern engineering projects use wind, water, steam and electricity power.

Inside pyramids, traps were often built to stop robbers reaching the tomb chamber where the body lay.

Great Pyramid of Giza
This pyramid was made of 2.3 million stone blocks weighing over 2 tonnes. It took 100,000 men about 20 years to build.

Stone blocks were dragged up ramps of earth on rollers. Afterwards the ramps were torn down.

Goldsmiths and bricklayers
Egyptian wall paintings show a wide range of craftsmen, from metalworkers and potters to carvers of ivory. Pyramids were often filled with goods such as chariots and fine furniture for use in the afterlife.

189

THE RIVER NILE

Gift of the Nile

The Greek historian Herodotus called Egypt 'the gift of the Nile'. Every year, as the mountain snow melted in the south, the world's longest river flooded, leaving a thick layer of mud on both sides of its banks. This made it possible to produce at least two, and often three, crops a year. The main crops were wheat for bread, and barley for beer. Flax and cotton were grown to make clothing. The people ate a lot of beans, figs, dates, garlic and salad vegetables.

Raising water
This cheap and simple device called a shaduf used a counterweight of stone or mud to lever up water from one level to the next. It is still in use today.

The Nile Delta
For most of its length the banks of the Nile were fertile for only a few kilometres either side before desert took over. But as the river neared the sea, it fanned out to make a delta 240 km wide. This marshy region was rich in fish and wildfowl, varying the local diet. Marshy areas yielded reeds, which were woven to make baskets, ropes, sleeping mats, shoes and even boats.

Irrigation
Egyptian farmers became expert in digging and controlling complex systems of canals, basins, dams and tanks to distribute and store the water of the great river. The water could then be used to best effect.

Rich harvest

All land was, in theory, owned by the pharaoh. The pharaoh looked after his people by setting aside some of each year's grain crop in huge stores, to control distribution. If the harvest failed, this grain could be used to make up the shortfall and prevent famine.

Egypt's lifeline

The Nile held Egypt together. Without the cheap method of transport the river provided, it would not have been possible for Thebes and Luxor to grow into great cities, as they relied on food being transported over long distances. Reeds growing along the banks of the river yielded papyrus on which records of taxes and grain stores were kept.

LEARNING TO WRITE

Early writing systems

Ancient Iraq and Egypt developed writing systems to record information about taxes, land grants, religious beliefs and histories. With writing they could also send letters to other rulers, record treaties and make inscriptions on buildings and in public places. Iraq's writing system, known as cuneiform, was based on wedge-shaped marks in clay tablets. In Egypt, a kind of paper was made from papyrus and scribes wrote with reed pens, using black and red inks.

Writing in pictures
Egyptian hieroglyphs stood for objects or sounds. About 700 were in common use but there were over 6000 in all. Hieroglyphs could be written from right to left, left to right, and up and down.

Schooling for boys
Scribes usually took their own sons as pupils. It took years to master hieroglyphs so fewer than one in 200 Egyptians were fully literate.

The Rosetta Stone
Discovered in Egypt in 1799, the Rosetta Stone carried an inscription that said the same thing in hieroglyphs (top), in a simplified hieroglyphic script called demotic (middle) and in ancient Greek (bottom).

Making paper
Paper was made by sticking together layers of strips made from the pith of the papyrus reed. Papyrus lasted, so it was good for keeping records on. It became one of Egypt's main exports.

Breaking codes

Before the discovery of the Rosetta Stone (above), the secret of reading hieroglyphs had been lost. The French Jean-Francois Champollion and the English Thomas Young puzzled out the answer between them by comparing the Greek text on the stone (which they could read) with the two Egyptian texts.

LIFE AFTER DEATH

Tending the dead

Egyptians preserved the bodies of their dead. It was essential that the body did not decay so that body and spirit could be reunited in the afterlife. At first they buried bodies in the desert sand, where they dried out. But jackals often dug up the bodies to eat. So they began putting them in wooden boxes or wicker baskets. However, this separated the body from the hot, dry sand, which killed off bacteria, so the bodies rotted. After centuries of trial and error an effective method of preserving bodies was developed.

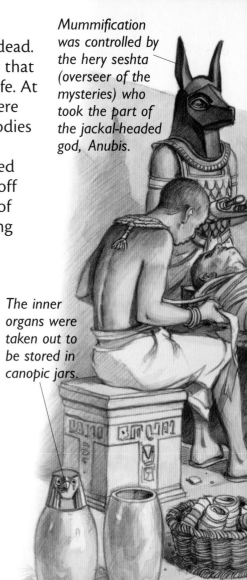

Mummification was controlled by the hery seshta (overseer of the mysteries) who took the part of the jackal-headed god, Anubis.

The inner organs were taken out to be stored in canopic jars.

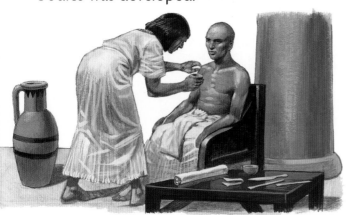

National health

The government paid doctors to give free treatment to travellers and soldiers at war. Egyptian doctors specialized in treating different parts of the body. The pharaoh had a different doctor for each eye!

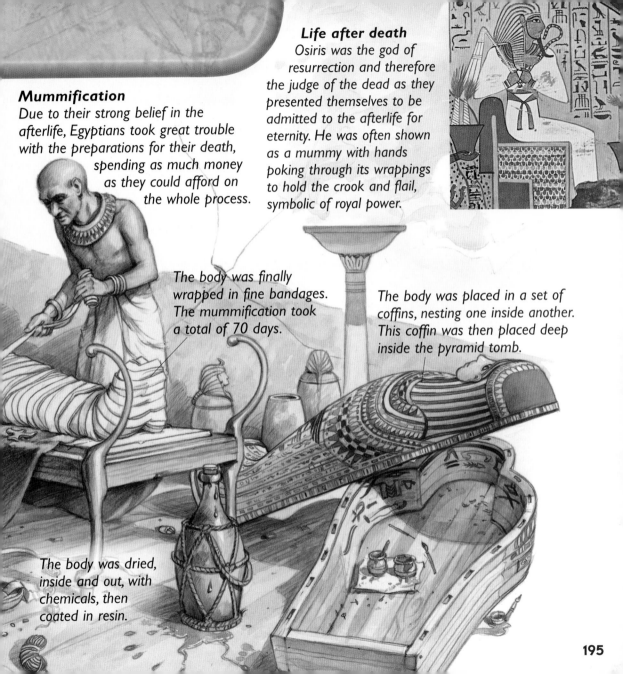

Mummification

Due to their strong belief in the afterlife, Egyptians took great trouble with the preparations for their death, spending as much money as they could afford on the whole process.

Life after death

Osiris was the god of resurrection and therefore the judge of the dead as they presented themselves to be admitted to the afterlife for eternity. He was often shown as a mummy with hands poking through its wrappings to hold the crook and flail, symbolic of royal power.

The body was finally wrapped in fine bandages. The mummification took a total of 70 days.

The body was placed in a set of coffins, nesting one inside another. This coffin was then placed deep inside the pyramid tomb.

The body was dried, inside and out, with chemicals, then coated in resin.

HONOURING THE GODS

For gods and heroes

Much Greek art was intended to honour gods or great leaders through sculpture or painting. Battles, real or legendary, were a favourite subject. Statues were made for temples and public squares. Paintings on wood, leather, textiles and the walls of rooms have almost all perished. Only paintings on vases have survived in any quantity because the paint was baked into the clay. Although a few of the greatest artists were respected, most were regarded as no better than common craftsmen because they worked with their hands like a potter or a shoemaker.

Carpet of stones
Mosaic pavements became increasingly common in wealthy Greek houses from the 4th century BC onwards. Under the Romans they were mass-produced for use in public buildings such as baths.

Ideal form
These columns of the Temple of Nike, goddess of victory, on the Acropolis in Athens, show the Greek taste for balance, symmetry and proportion – the style that Europeans came to think of as Classical.

196

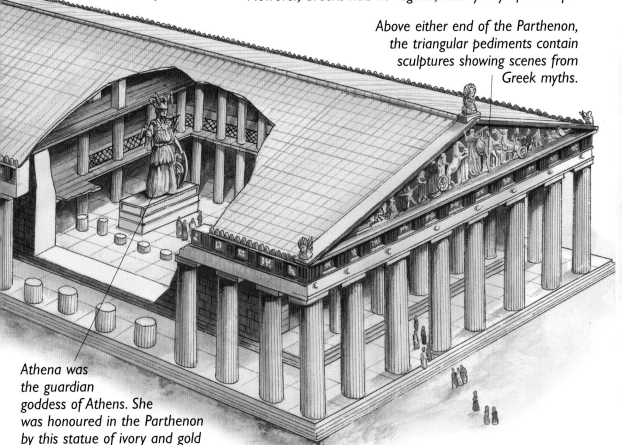

Wise owl
Early Greek coins usually carried a symbol of the city that minted them. The owl of wisdom was the emblem of Athena.

The Parthenon
On a hilltop above Athens stood the Parthenon, a white marble temple. Temples did have priests, but worship could also be led by the head of a family. The Greeks, like other peoples, had festivals where the whole community worshipped together in the temple. However, Greeks had no regular, weekly day of worship.

Above either end of the Parthenon, the triangular pediments contain sculptures showing scenes from Greek myths.

Athena was the guardian goddess of Athens. She was honoured in the Parthenon by this statue of ivory and gold which stood over 18 m high.

EARLY MEDICINE

The birth of medicine

Doctors in ancient Greece understood the importance of diet, rest, massage and exercise. They knew how to use drugs to relieve pain, to give sleep and to make people vomit. They could set broken bones and bleed out poisons. They also knew that surgery was usually a risky last resort – patients who did not die of shock and loss of blood often died from infection afterwards. Separate systems of medicine developed in ancient China and India, but shared the same general view of the importance of diet, the use of drugs and the dangers of surgery.

Doctors in all three systems also believed in astrology – that the movements of the stars and planets could tell when the best time was to use a particular form of treatment.

The Hippocratic Oath

Hippocrates, a Greek doctor of the 4th century BC, drew up an oath binding doctors only to use their skill to heal patients and never to harm them. As a doctor, Hippocrates taught the importance of fresh air, cleanliness and a balanced diet. He also knew it was important to keep a record of each individual's illness and how it developed.

Lessons in medicine

All educated men had some knowledge of medicine, which they learnt alongside other subjects, including sport. Specialist doctors trained at medical schools like the one on the island of Kos, where Hippocrates taught.

The four humours

Greek medical theory believed that good health depended on a proper balance between the four body fluids – blood, phlegm, yellow bile and black bile. If there was too much or too little of one, the patient would suffer in body or mind until the balance had been corrected by treatment such as sweating, bleeding or vomiting. This idea remained the backbone of medical thinking in Europe until the great scientific advances of the 16th and 17th centuries.

The gladiators' doctor

Greek medical knowledge was summed up by Galen who lived in the 2nd century AD. He went to Rome and became personal doctor to three Roman emperors. Galen was the first to use the pulse as a way of finding out about a patient's condition. His teachings helped others to learn for more than one thousand years after his death. Galen's theories were based on what he learnt from his early experience as surgeon to gladiators.

The healing god

Asclepius was the Greek and Roman god of healing. His sign, a staff and serpent, is still often used as the badge of medical organizations.

199

Power struggles

Greek legends of gods and heroes were full of tales of war. Real life was just as full of battles. The city states of ancient Greece were often at war with each other. Sparta was organized entirely on military lines. The most famous leaders of the rich trading city of Athens were also able soldiers. Sparta and Athens destroyed each other's power in a long war. Under its warrior leader, Philip II, the kingdom of Macedonia to the north conquered all the city states of mainland Greece to unite them against the mighty Persian Empire.

Alexander the Great

Son of Philip II, Alexander (356–323 BC) carried out his father's plan to conquer Persia and led his armies as far as India before turning back. He founded the port of Alexandria in Egypt and many other cities, but his empire fell apart after his early death.

Great thinkers

The Greeks were intensely curious about the world around them. The great teacher Socrates (469–399 BC, left) wrote nothing, but his method of learning through questioning was recorded by his pupil Plato (428–347 BC). Plato's main interest was politics. His pupil, Aristotle (384–322 BC, right) was interested in everything, from politics to plants and even planets. Aristotle was, in turn, Alexander the Great's tutor.

Alexander's coins

Although Alexander's empire died with him, his coinage lived on – a lasting symbol of power. From Macedonia to Babylon his mints had turned out a vast quantity of coins of uniform types and weights. They spread the idea that coins should carry a ruler's name. Soon coins carried their portrait as well.

Wall of spears

Greeks fought as compact bodies (phalanxes) of heavily armed infantry in ranks up to eight deep. Their main weapon was a long spear. It was almost impossible to give changes of orders in the din of battle. The skill of a great leader like Alexander the Great was in choosing the lie of the land to give his army the best advantage before fighting actually began.

THE OLYMPIC GAMES

The competitors
Only men were allowed to compete in the Olympic Games. Women were not even allowed to be present as spectators. There were separate games for women, although these only involved running races.

Playing to win
Many Greek athletes were professionals, specializing in a single event. As there were many lesser events, apart from the Olympics, they could make a living by travelling from one to another.

Judges and rules
Cheating was severely punished by the judges. In ancient Greece, only slaves could normally be beaten as a punishment. But cheats at the Games could also be made to pay for sacrifices to the gods.

Perfect bodies
Ancient Greeks thought the athlete was a symbol of human perfection.

The Olympic Games

Ancient Greece consisted of some 300 city states, which were often at war with each other. Young men undertook training to make them fit for fighting. Sporting competitions such as running, wrestling, chariot-racing and throwing the javelin developed as a result. The first Olympic Games were held in 776 BC. The Greeks divided time itself into the four-year periods, which separated each Olympiad from the last. During the Games there was a truce in all wars so that contestants and spectators could travel to the Games. The Greeks saw the Games as an exhibition of courage, fitness and the beauty of the human body.

Prizes for the winners

Sporting heroes were rewarded with jars of olive oil or laurel wreaths as prizes. The real prize was fame and the glory it brought to a winner's home city. Sporting heroes were often honoured by their fellow citizens with statues, pensions and free meals for life.

A trip to the theatre

Greek drama included both tragedies and comedies. Actors wore masks and were often accompanied by a chorus and music. Greek open-air theatres provided entertainment for up to 12,000 people. They had superb acoustics so that even people sitting right at the back could hear clearly.

203

ROMAN EMPERORS

Debating skills

The senators discussed laws and government plans in the courtroom. Ambitious young Romans learnt rhetoric, the art of persuasive public speaking. Many of their teachers were Greeks.

Power

Even though the power of the Senate declined under the Empire, its magnificent buildings and solemn debates made it seem as if it still had influence.

The Senate

When Rome was a republic (before 31 BC), the Senate was the most powerful part of the government and it remained an important advisory body when it was ruled by emperors. Augustus set membership at 600. Senators were mostly large landowners. The most influential came from ancient, noble families. As the power of emperors increased, the Senate's direct powers of government became limited to Rome itself. Rule by emperors led to civil wars as ambitious generals used their soldiers to seize the imperial throne by force.

A helping hand

As large landowners and heads of families, senators were expected to look after the interests of their tenants in law cases, and find jobs in the army or government service for their relatives.

The accused

He could be forced to attend court if necessary.

Emperors and empire

The Roman republic fell in a power struggle between Julius Caesar and his enemies. They murdered Caesar in 43 BC but were then defeated by his adopted son and heir, who became Rome's first emperor, Augustus, in 27 BC. The empire reached its peak under the first non-Roman to become emperor, Trajan, a Spanish soldier. In 395, Diocletian split the empire into two halves. The eastern half became the powerful empire of Byzantium, bordered by another powerful empire, Persia.

Room to view
Interested citizens could watch from the viewing gallery.

Senate factions
Senators gathered in this hall before entering a courtroom.

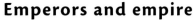

Face of power
Romans knew which government they were living under from what appeared on the coinage. Under the republic, coins bore pictures of Roman gods; under the empire, portraits of emperors.

Great thinkers

The Romans were less interested than the Greeks in abstract ideas. The best Roman thinkers excelled in history and the law. Cicero (106–43 BC) studied rhetoric for three years in Greece and became a brilliantly successful lawyer, writer and politician – until he was executed!

Augustus Caesar
Augustus was a brilliant organizer. He rebuilt Rome and gave it water supplies, a fire brigade and police force. Augustus also reformed the Senate and army, and founded a navy. The system of government that he created lasted for two centuries after his death.

High-rise homes

The Romans invented apartment blocks called insulae that had three or four storeys. They were mostly for poor people who made up the bulk of Rome's population of over one million. The blocks were well serviced, but fire was a constant danger in the overcrowded insulae, as people often cooked meals in their rooms. Many blocks had a cookshop at the ground-floor level, selling fast food.

Hygiene for health

The Romans understood the need for hygiene and proper sanitation in crowded cities to prevent disease. Public toilets were built over channels of running water to flush away the waste.

Home entertainment

The wealthy gave banquets for friends. Nine was considered the ideal number for a dinner party. Guests ate lying on their sides on couches. Entertainment was provided by professional dancers, singers, jugglers, acrobats or conjurers.

Luxurious living

While poor city-dwellers lived in crowded apartments, the rich lived in extravagant villas. Poor people went to the public baths and drew water from public fountains. Rich people had their own bathroom suites, piped water and underfloor heating. High walls, string gates and small outer windows gave villas security and concealed the wealth within. Fine Roman roads enabled the rich to travel to second homes at the seaside or in the country.

Carried away

Wealthy women and old or sick people travelled in curtained litters carried by a team of slaves.

ROMAN ENGINEERING

Inventive engineering

The Romans used the styles of architecture developed by the Greeks, whose temples they greatly admired. Many great engineering projects were the work of the Roman army. In Britain, Roman soldiers built Hadrian's Wall, which runs 117 km from one side of the country to the other. Enormous public bath-houses with complicated plumbing and heating systems were a major feature of every sizeable Roman town. The actual running of baths, amphitheatres, aqueducts and other public facilities usually relied on the labour of slaves.

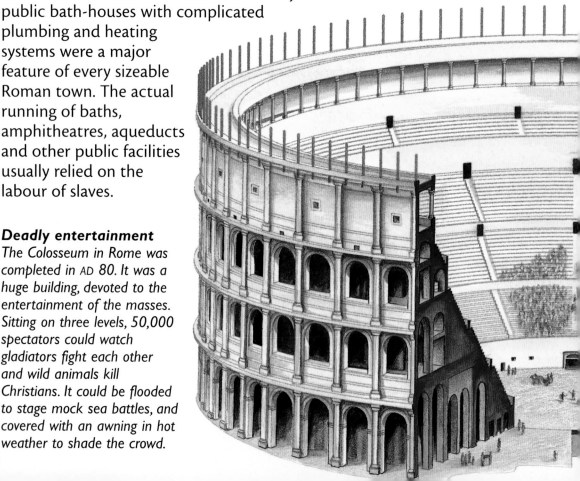

Deadly entertainment

The Colosseum in Rome was completed in AD 80. It was a huge building, devoted to the entertainment of the masses. Sitting on three levels, 50,000 spectators could watch gladiators fight each other and wild animals kill Christians. It could be flooded to stage mock sea battles, and covered with an awning in hot weather to shade the crowd.

Water transportation

With one million inhabitants, Rome needed huge volumes of water for drinking, cooking, washing, bathing and industry. By AD 97, nine aqueducts brought in 320 million litres of water a day from mountain springs.

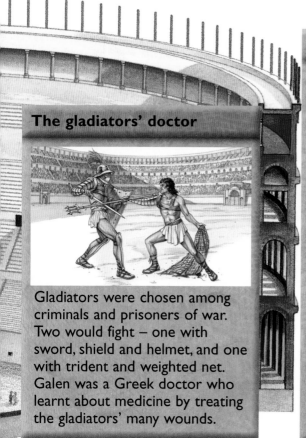

The gladiators' doctor

Gladiators were chosen among criminals and prisoners of war. Two would fight – one with sword, shield and helmet, and one with trident and weighted net. Galen was a Greek doctor who learnt about medicine by treating the gladiators' many wounds.

Roman road building

Curved road surfaces helped rain run off

Mileposts were set up to mark distances between towns

Roman roads were built using a system of graded materials in layers. The more the roads were used, the harder the surface became because the weight of the traffic compressed the layers together.

THE ROMAN ARMY

Organized manpower

The Roman army originally
consisted of native Roman citizens, but
as the empire expanded, it took in men
from conquered territories. The army was
divided into legions of roughly 6000 men,
which had the full range of skills to fight
as independent units. Roman troops were
extremely well-drilled and trained and
frequently beat armies far larger in number
through sheer discipline and method. The
Roman army was extremely well-organized,
like most areas of life in the Roman Empire.

Battle gear
Roman soldiers in close combat used a short,
heavy stabbing sword. They protected themselves
with a long, curved shield, flexible body armour
and close-fitting helmet contoured to ward off
blows to the face and neck.

Camp building
A Roman legion included trained masons,
carpenters and surveyors. Here they are shown
constructing a powerful stone fortress as a
defensive base. They could also put up camps
of wood and earth in a few hours.

The Roman soldier

The core of the army consisted of long-service professional soldiers trained to fight as heavily armed infantry. Roman soldiers on the march cooked for themselves in groups of ten, sharing the same tent. Each legionary was expected to carry 132 kg of weapons, supplies and equipment.

Cavalry officer

Legionary
A soldier carried all his equipment and supplies with him on a march.

Protective shell
Legionaries facing a barrage of stones, or a shower of spears and arrows, would form a testudo (tortoise) to protect themselves while advancing to close combat.

THE FIRST BOOKS

Precious books

In medieval Europe books were written on vellum, a very fine parchment made from the skin of a calf, kid or lamb. Preparing a single sheet of vellum took many hours of careful scraping and softening. To make a copy of the New Testament of the Bible used three hundred lambs' skins. As it might also take three years for a scribe to copy out the text, books were incredibly precious. A monastery with fifty books would have had a large library. Monasteries loaned books to each other so that they could be copied.

Team effort
Making a book needed the skills of many craftsmen to prepare vellum, ink and pens, to write the text, to paint illuminations and to make a cover of wood and leather.

Illumination

Books were illuminated with brilliantly coloured initial letters and drawings in the margin. These were not just for decoration, but acted as markers to help the reader find particular passages of text.

212

Tales of gods

Vikings had little use for books and writing but loved tales of battles and monsters. So Viking bards memorized long poems, called sagas, about their gods and heroes.

Book of Kells

This ornamented gospel probably began on the Scottish island of Iona in the 8th century. After Viking raids began in 795 the book was taken to Kells in Ireland to be completed safely.

MEDIEVAL WARFARE

Devastation by fire

Throughout the Middle Ages, war, not peace, was the normal state of affairs throughout Europe. After the break-up of the Roman Empire in the 5th century, Christian Europe was tormented by raids and invasions by Muslims from the south, Vikings from the north and pagan Balts, Letts and Magyars from the east. In later centuries strong kingdoms declared war on each other to enlarge their territories. The most widely used weapon was fire – immensely destructive to homes and barns made of wood, and fields full of grain. The Church tried to limit the damage by teaching that priests and other innocent people should be spared from harm.

Mantlet

Crossbowman

Longboat explorers
Viking raiders from Scandinavia were great seafarers who sailed around Western Europe in open longboats, pillaging for treasure and slaves. Later, Vikings settled in England, Normandy and the Scottish Islands.

Under siege

Sieges, rather than battles, were the most
common form of medieval warfare. Castles were
rarely taken by storm and could usually hold out,
providing they had enough food and water. Besieging armies
were often destroyed by disease and desertion.

Mangonels batter rocks
against castle walls while
wooden assault towers, built
for use during a seige, are
wheeled up against them.

Siege
tower

Scaling
ladder

Mangonel

EPIDEMICS

Killer epidemics

An epidemic is an outbreak of disease bad enough to wipe out a whole community. Ancient Greece, Rome and Byzantium all suffered epidemics that killed millions and terrified survivors by their scale and suddenness. Infections spread quickly among people living close together in crowded, dirty conditions, with poor sanitation. Epidemics led to deserted cities and abandoned fields as people fled to the safety of unaffected areas. This often led to famine as fields of crops were left to die. It could take decades or even centuries for populations to recover to former levels.

Bubonic plague
Bites from the fleas carried in the fur of rats spread the bubonic plague. An even more deadly form, pneumonic plague, could be caught by breathing in droplets from the breath of an infected person.

Disappearing children

The Pied Piper was said to have charmed away rats from Hamelin in Germany. Refused payment, he also charmed away the town's children. The legend may record an epidemic of child deaths.

Leprosy warning

There were epidemics of leprosy in Europe in the 1100s and 1200s. Leprosy, a contagious skin disease, was not usually fatal like the plague, but its unfortunate sufferers often carried clappers to warn others to stay away.

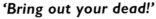

'Bring out your dead!'

When plague broke out, a red cross was painted on the door of the sufferer to warn people. At night, a cart collected the dead bodies.

MERCHANTS

Tales from abroad
Marco Polo (below) wrote a famous account of travelling to China and living there between 1271 and 1295. He described China as a huge, rich empire with strange wonders unknown in Europe such as paper money and a stone that burned – coal! It is possible he never actually went there himself and just copied other travellers' tales. His book still made many Europeans eager to seek their fortunes abroad.

Tails from abroad
Between 1405 and 1433, Admiral Zheng He (above) led seven fleets of junks from China to bring back gifts, goods and animals from abroad, including the first giraffe seen in China. His last voyage reached East Africa. Zheng He's junks were built with special watertight compartments to stop them sinking if they became holed in one place.

Precious cargoes

Cloves

Long-distance trade and travel between Europe and Asia revived slowly after the break-up of the Roman Empire in the 5th century AD. The high costs and risks of travel at this time limited long-distance trade to very valuable goods, such as gemstones, gold, silk, porcelain and carpets. Muslim merchants in the Middle East came to link Europe, Asia and Africa. Muslims shared a common language, Arabic, and common laws, which made trading easier for them. New technologies spread along trade routes. Paper-making was invented in China in the 2nd century BC. The secret took a thousand years to reach the Arab world and another six centuries to get to northern Europe.

Keeping count

During the 5th century, merchants were usually the only people controlling distribution of goods. They were also the only ones who could read and write, apart from priests, with Chinese and Arabic used as the main trading languages.

Trade goods

Spices for food, dyes for cloth and drugs for medicine were the most common goods traded over long distances. The most popular spices were pepper, cloves, nutmeg and cinnamon. Most spices came from southern India and Indonesia.

Importing ideas

Until about 1700, Europeans did not know how to make porcelain so they imported it from China and Japan. As well as being beautiful, porcelain is light and heat proof. Porcelain bowls became even more popular when Europeans began to drink tea.

RESOURCEFUL FARMING

Farming to live

From 1200–1600, European villagers produced most of their own food. In addition, they needed to grow extra crops or fatten animals for sale at the local market. The profit they made could buy iron or salt, things they could not make at home.

Serfdom

Most farmers were serfs. They paid rent on their land by working two or three days a week for the lord who owned their village.

Thatching

Straw gathered from the fields could be used to thatch roofs.

Non-intensive farming

Labour was carried out using only the power of humans and animals. This did not allow the farmer to farm the land intensively.

Recycling

Pigs and poultry were very useful to villagers because they could survive on kitchen scraps and waste.

Sheepshearing

Sheep provided wool to be made into cloth and meat to be eaten. Their milk could be made into cheese, their bones boiled for glue and their horns made into spoons.

PILGRIMAGES

Religious relics

Relics of saints, in the form of personal belongings or pieces of their bones, were often kept by the faithful. A popular relic was in the shape of the Christian symbol of the cross.

Telling tales

The most famous place of pilgrimage in England was Canterbury Cathedral, where the body of St Thomas à Becket was buried. The poet Geoffrey Chaucer (died 1400) wrote The Canterbury Tales, a series of stories in verse. The tales were supposed to have been told by a party of pilgrims to pass the time on their long journey from London to Canterbury Cathedral.

Pilgrimages in Europe

A pilgrimage is a journey to a holy place. Christians went on pilgrimage to holy places to ask God for forgiveness from sins, to beg to be healed from an illness or to have a child, or even to give thanks for good fortune. Pilgrimage was the nearest thing there was to a holiday. Although it had a serious purpose, it also meant seeing new places, meeting new people and buying souvenirs. Some famous pilgrimage places were Jerusalem, Rome and Santiago de Compostela in Spain.

Pilgrimages in Asia

Pilgrimage is also part of the Muslim, Hindu and Buddhist religions. A famous Buddhist pilgrimage route on the Japanese island of Shikoku involved visiting 88 shrines. Another Buddhist pilgrimage was to Kandy in Sri Lanka where it was said there was one of the Buddha's teeth preserved as a relic. Hindus gathered in huge numbers each year at Varanasi to bathe in the waters of the sacred river Ganges. Each year Muslims went on a pilgrimage to Mecca in Arabia, the birthplace of the prophet Muhammad. Afterwards they often visited Medina, where he is buried. Meeting other pilgrims from many different places was an efficient way of spreading news to tell when they returned home.

Safety in numbers
Pilgrims often travelled in groups, partly for company and partly for protection against bandits. The picture above shows Muslim pilgrims leaving Egypt for Mecca. They are being given a noisy send-off by a military band.

MEDIEVAL BUILDERS

Light of faith

The brightly coloured stained glass windows of medieval cathedrals created a dazzling light show as the sun shifted round the building in the course of a day. Priests used the Bible stories that the windows showed to teach worshippers who could not read or write.

Community effort

Building a castle or palace showed the power of a ruler. Building a cathedral showed the wealth of a community. Most took centuries to complete.

An apprentice learns the skills of his trade.

Glass was made as it was needed.

Strips of lead are join to hold the glass in place.

A glazier cuts glass to the shape required to fit the window.

Finally, the glazed panels are placed in the stone frame.

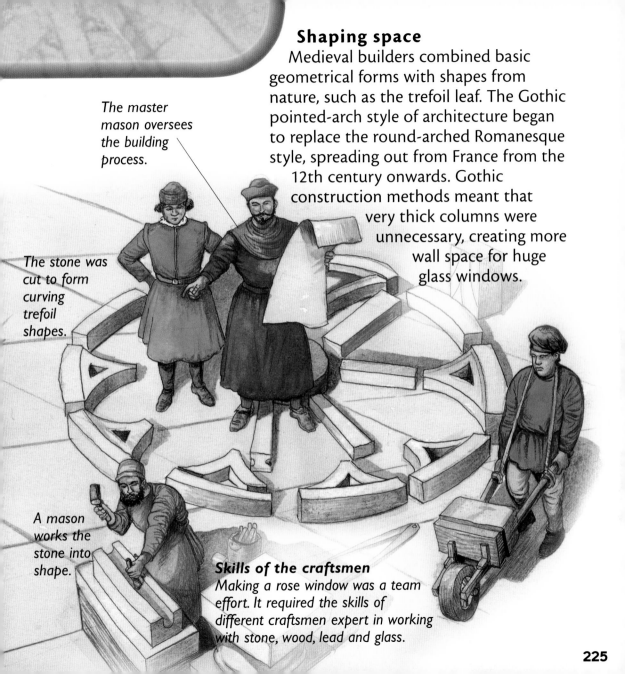

Shaping space

Medieval builders combined basic geometrical forms with shapes from nature, such as the trefoil leaf. The Gothic pointed-arch style of architecture began to replace the round-arched Romanesque style, spreading out from France from the 12th century onwards. Gothic construction methods meant that very thick columns were unnecessary, creating more wall space for huge glass windows.

The master mason oversees the building process.

The stone was cut to form curving trefoil shapes.

A mason works the stone into shape.

Skills of the craftsmen

Making a rose window was a team effort. It required the skills of different craftsmen expert in working with stone, wood, lead and glass.

MEDIEVAL HOMES

Home discomforts

Most medieval homes were built on a framework of wooden timbers, with walls of mud smeared over panels of woven sticks. Roofs were made of thick thatch, an ideal home for birds, rats and insects. Floors were made of trodden earth. Windows were covered with oiled parchment, which let light through. Smoke from an open fire escaped as best it could. Furniture consisted of rough wooden benches, stools and trestle-tables. Possessions were stored in chests or on pegs and shelves. Dirt and damp were normal and just got worse in winter.

Music for the home

When bad weather kept people indoors they amused themselves with telling tales and asking riddles. Rich people listened to professional minstrels who sang, played and recited stories in verse.

Living with livestock

Chickens and pigs were kept near the house to be fed on kitchen waste. In winter, oxen and cows were often brought inside to stop them from freezing or being stolen. Their body heat helped to keep the house warm.

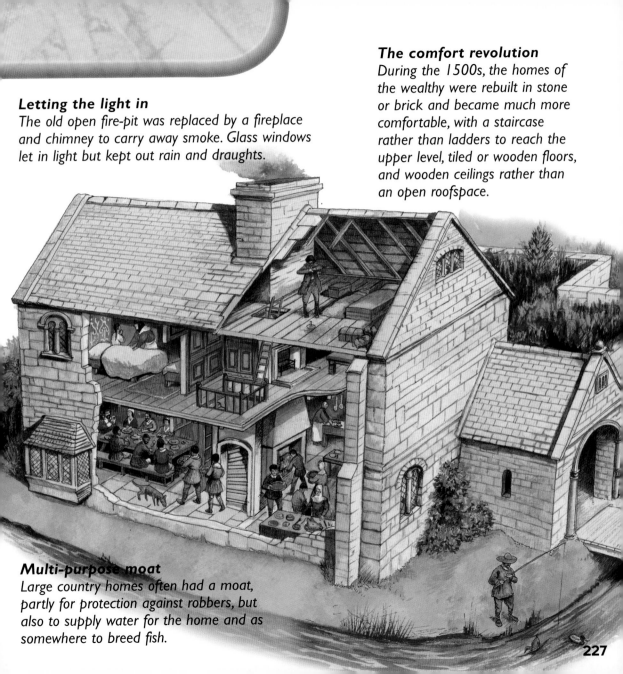

Letting the light in
The old open fire-pit was replaced by a fireplace and chimney to carry away smoke. Glass windows let in light but kept out rain and draughts.

The comfort revolution
During the 1500s, the homes of the wealthy were rebuilt in stone or brick and became much more comfortable, with a staircase rather than ladders to reach the upper level, tiled or wooden floors, and wooden ceilings rather than an open roofspace.

Multi-purpose moat
Large country homes often had a moat, partly for protection against robbers, but also to supply water for the home and as somewhere to breed fish.

227

MEDIEVAL FUN

Country pursuits

Plays and operas could normally only be seen in the palaces of kings or in big cities. However, when theatres were closed on account of the plague, companies of actors took their plays out to the countryside. Most people lived in small towns or villages and shared the same outdoor pleasures. The rich had the leisure to hunt or dance any day they liked. But most people worked long hours and only had time off on holy days or traditional festivals such as May Day, which marked the coming of summer.

War practice
Hunting put food on the table and was also good practice for war. Hunters kept fit and learnt how to ride well and to use bows and spears skilfully.

The Globe Theatre
In Shakespeare's day London's theatres were outside the city walls. The Globe could cram in 3000 people, most of them standing. The growth of professional theatre marked the beginning of entertainment as business.

Holiday fun
Special fairs were held on holidays. Dancing round the maypole was usual on May Day. Baiting bears and bulls with dogs was a popular entertainment.

Favourite sports
Although bows and arrows were no longer used in war, archery remained a popular sport. So did wrestling, and fighting with cudgels and quarter-staffs.

MONARCHS

The cult of Elizabeth
Elizabeth I developed the image of a strong, glittering, virgin queen, which she stamped on the minds of her people and on her property, including her coins.

Widespread monarchy

The normal form of government in this period, from Europe to China, was monarchy. The republican city states of Italy and the cantons of Switzerland were unusual exceptions. Most rulers increased their power at the expense of elected parliaments or assemblies of nobles. England was rather different. Conflicts between rulers and parliaments came to show that the country was stronger when they worked together and the monarch's power was eroded.

Monarchy or Republic?
Charles I (1625–1649) tried to rule England without the support of the Parliament. This plunged the country into civil war. Charles lost and was executed in 1649. England became the Commonwealth, a republic. This collapsed with the death of its leader, Oliver Cromwell. In 1660 Charles I's son was restored to the throne as Charles II.

Spies
Every ruler feared plots against them. Elizabeth I's trusted minister, Francis Walsingham, created Europe's first modern spy service. His well-educated agents worked to uncover traitors of the queen.

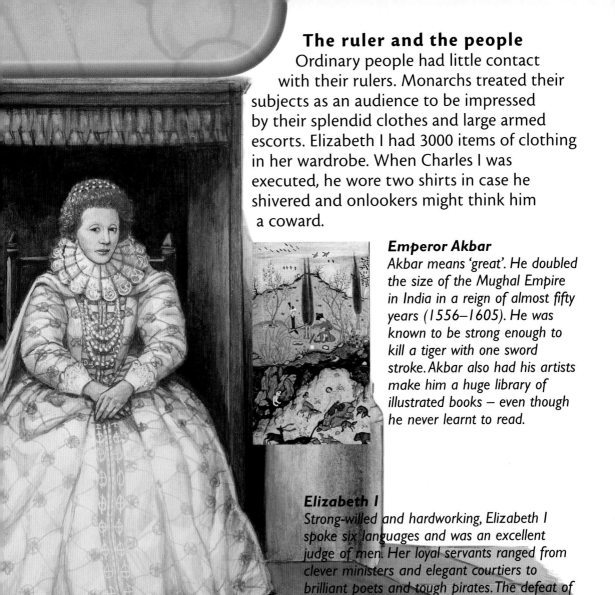

The ruler and the people

Ordinary people had little contact with their rulers. Monarchs treated their subjects as an audience to be impressed by their splendid clothes and large armed escorts. Elizabeth I had 3000 items of clothing in her wardrobe. When Charles I was executed, he wore two shirts in case he shivered and onlookers might think him a coward.

Emperor Akbar

Akbar means 'great'. He doubled the size of the Mughal Empire in India in a reign of almost fifty years (1556–1605). He was known to be strong enough to kill a tiger with one sword stroke. Akbar also had his artists make him a huge library of illustrated books – even though he never learnt to read.

Elizabeth I

Strong-willed and hardworking, Elizabeth I spoke six languages and was an excellent judge of men. Her loyal servants ranged from clever ministers and elegant courtiers to brilliant poets and tough pirates. The defeat of the great Spanish Armada by her navy in 1588 made the English feel that 'Good Queen Bess' had God's special protection.

PERILOUS JOURNEYS

Protection from pirates
Pirates flourished where they could hide away on small offshore islands and come out to prey on isolated merchant ships. The South China Seas and the Caribbean were ideal for pirates. Merchant ships started to sail heavily armed for protection and often in convoys. Pirates finally lost their grip on the seas with the arrival of fast steamboats, which could hunt the pirates down or just outrun them.

Bandits
Travellers usually went in groups to protect themselves from robbers. When bandits were caught, they were often hanged at the scene of their crime as a warning to others.

Stagecoach travel
A return to Roman methods of road-making, using graded layers of stones, made it possible to run regular inter-city horse-drawn coach services. By 1830, British stagecoaches were averaging 13 km/h, carrying mail and passengers.

Reluctant road menders
Local people were often forced to mend the roads passing through their area and so did the job badly. After all, it was strangers who would benefit most.

Carts for the market
Broad-wheeled carts could carry heavy loads to local markets but only went at about 5 km/h.

The dangers of road travel

Compared to Roman times, roads before 1800 were poorly made and badly maintained. Travel was often uncomfortable, tiring and dangerous even in good weather, and sometimes quite impossible in winter. Carriages were only for the wealthy, women, the old and the sick. Most people walked. Apart from trade, the main reason for travelling was pilgrimage to holy places. Kings and rich people travelled to their different estates to live and hunt.

Postman on horse
Governments used messengers on horseback to speed the spread of news by delivering dispatches about major events.

Pedlars
Pedlars walked from village to village selling small things such as needles and ribbons. They also helped the spread of news by gossiping about the outside world, often unreliably.

233

PALACES AND THEATRES

The Sun King

Louis XIV liked to see himself as a brilliant centre around which the world, or at least his court, revolved, as the planets revolved round the Sun. Louis used the Sun as a symbol of power.

Dazzling palaces

At five years old, Louis XIV (1638–1715) became king of France, the richest and most powerful country in Europe. In fact Louis declared, "I am the State," and set about showing off his wealth and glory through extravagance in all things. Royal factories and workshops were founded to produce furniture, clocks and ceramics to decorate the king's palaces. At Versailles, outside Paris, from 1669 onwards Louis began building a royal residence, which dazzled all of Europe and was widely copied for a century.

The gardens of Versailles

The gardens around the palace of Versailles were laid out by master designer André Le Nôtre. He transformed a muddy swamp into majestic parks, woods and planted beds, full of statues and spectacular waterworks.

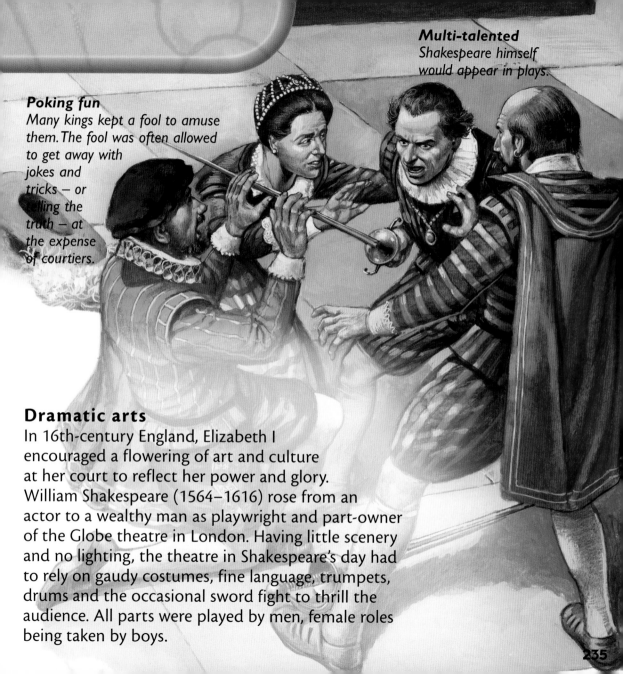

Poking fun
Many kings kept a fool to amuse
them. The fool was often allowed
to get away with
jokes and
tricks – or
telling the
truth – at
the expense
of courtiers.

Dramatic arts

In 16th-century England, Elizabeth I
encouraged a flowering of art and culture
at her court to reflect her power and glory.
William Shakespeare (1564–1616) rose from an
actor to a wealthy man as playwright and part-owner
of the Globe theatre in London. Having little scenery
and no lighting, the theatre in Shakespeare's day had
to rely on gaudy costumes, fine language, trumpets,
drums and the occasional sword fight to thrill the
audience. All parts were played by men, female roles
being taken by boys.

DISCOVERY BY SEA

Sail power

By 1400, ships used sails of different sizes and shapes so that they could move forwards even when the wind was not blowing directly that way. By 1500, Portuguese sailors had reached Brazil and found a sea route to India by sailing right round Africa. But storms and calms, changing winds and tides meant it was still impossible to say just how many days or months any journey would take.

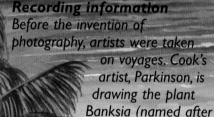

Recording information
Before the invention of photography, artists were taken on voyages. Cook's artist, Parkinson, is drawing the plant Banksia (named after Joseph Banks).

Navigation

The sailor's biggest problem was simply knowing his ship's location. This depended on having accurate instruments for making observations, measurements and calculations based on landmarks, winds, tides and the Sun, Moon and stars.

Telescope

Backstaff

Compass

The earliest locomotives were built to haul coal from mines to waterways. In 1830 a new line was opened to carry both goods and passengers between the city of Manchester and the port of Liverpool.

Captain Cook's adventures

Captain James Cook (1728–1779) of the Royal Navy mapped more of the world than any other single person. His exploration ships were originally built for the British coastal coal trade, but carried him on three great voyages round the world. Cook proved that New Zealand was two islands and not part of Australia. He was also the first seafarer to sail into Antarctic waters and prove that there was no great undiscovered 'Southern Continent'. Cook's voyages brought back a wealth of information about new territories.

Botanical Banks

Scientist Joseph Banks (1744–1820) sailed with Cook on his first voyage and brought back 3000 plants – 1400 of them were unknown to Europeans. He founded the Royal Botanic Gardens at Kew in England.

BUILDING STYLES

Building with wood

In countries with big forests, such as Norway or Japan, most buildings and bridges were made of wood rather than stone or brick. Ornamentation of buildings therefore required different skills of joinery, carving or patterning. Fires and damp have destroyed most old wooden structures, but some outstanding examples have survived for as long as 1200 years. In Japan, craftsmen used great skill in mixing hard and soft woods to make earthquake-proof buildings.

Handmade details

The Japanese emperors' badge is shaped like a chrysanthemum with sixteen petals. It therefore adorns many royal palaces.

All under one roof

The Batak people of Sumatra, Indonesia, live together in large family groups. The decorated wooden houses are traditionally held together with wooden pins instead of nails. The floor of the building is supported by wooden posts and the roof is tall and curved.

Stone for the wealthy

The expense of quarrying, transporting and carving stone meant that it was mostly used for important or special buildings such as castles, cathedrals, churches and palaces. Sometimes, less prominent buildings and walls were made cheaply in brick or cemented rubble and covered with an outer layer of stone.

Windsor Castle
Originally built by William the Conquerer in 1070, Windsor Castle is one of the residencies of the British monarchy. The castle has a round keep (tower), which stands at 30 m in height.

The Taj Mahal
This tomb for the wife of the Mughal emperor, Shah Jahan, was completed around 1650 at Agra in India. The Taj Mahal is built of white marble, inlaid with semi-precious stones. It took 20,000 men 20 years to build.

239

CIVIL WAR

Fighting with guns

The American Civil War (1861–1865) was one of the bloodiest conflicts of the 19th century. The Southern states were fighting an army from their own country for the right to withdraw from the Union of states that made up America. The Southerners wanted to form a separate Confederate States of America in order to preserve slavery. At the time when the war began, America had few professional soldiers. Fighting between untrained armies led to massive casualties.

Loading a musket
The single-shot musket was loaded using a ram-rod to tamp the ball and charge down the barrel. This had to be done standing up, exposing the soldier to enemy fire.

Modern war
The American Civil War has been described as the very first 'modern war'. It was basically a fight between two different philosophies of life – the forward-thinking, industrial, anti-slavery north versus the old-fashioned pro-slavery south, with its greater military resourses.

Industrial strength

The Union flag had stars for all the 13 original states. Not only could the Union (Northern) army rely on most of America's industry to supply it, but it could also draw on a far larger population for recruits.

Abraham Lincoln

In 1860, Abraham Lincoln, was elected as president. He was a great leader who helped bring slavery to an end. He was assassinated in 1865.

Lack of weapons

The Confederates had their own version of the Union flag, also with 13 stars. The Confederate (Southern) army had good leadership, but the industries in its power could not produce enough weapons and equipment for the men.

PRINTING

Multiple copies
Printing was first developed in Korea and China around the 8th century and used to make copies of Buddhist religious teachings and prayers. European printers first used carved wooden blocks to make cheap religious pictures to be sold to pilgrims as souvenirs. Printing from reusable metal was perfected in the mid-15th century by Johannes Gutenberg. William Caxton brought printing to England in 1476.

The printing industry
By 1850 in Europe and the United States, large printing workshops were printing and assembling thousands of copies of illustrated books and magazines in just a few days. The new steam-powered rotary presses introduced in 1846, could print 8000 sheets an hour.

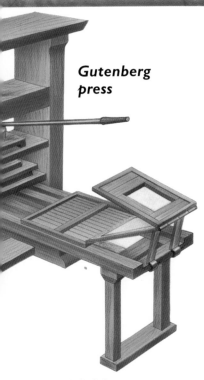

Gutenberg press

Spreading news

The earliest type of press used a screw mechanism, like a press for squeezing the juice from grapes or olives. It was slow to operate. Later a counterweight was invented, designed to lift the printing-plate automatically after each sheet was printed. This press was three times faster. As a result it became possible to print thousands of daily newspapers quickly. The first daily papers appeared in Germany in the 1660s.

Art and advertising

The Japanese were the first to master multi-coloured printing using carved wooden blocks from around 1740. Coloured prints were used to advertise plays and restaurants or to depict travel scenes for sale as souvenirs. These prints were not thought of as great art at the time, as they are now.

Printed Bible

The invention of printing made it possible to produce a Bible for a tenth of the price of a handwritten copy and a hundred times as fast. Cheap printed Bibles put religion into the hands of ordinary people and helped spread Protestantism in Europe.

INDUSTRIAL CITIES

Coketown

Charles Dickens' Coketown was an imaginary industrial city in one of Britain's manufacturing regions. He described it as permanently shrouded in smoke and smeared with soot from factory chimneys. Coal had created a whole new way of life. It drove the steam engines that powered factories and locomotives. It made the bricks for buildings and provided the gas that lit them. Coal fires heated homes and boiled the water for washing, cooking and bathing. Coal made the iron used for many everyday things, from railways to frying pans. Coal was essential to keep a home warm and comfortable but the housewife's life was a constant battle against the filth it created. However, this air pollution, along with foul water supplies and dirty drains, meant town dwellers lived with the constant threat of an epidemic.

Home, sweet home?
As more work was done in factories rather than home workshops, the worlds of work and home became more separate. But without buses or bicycles most people had to live within walking distance of the factory. This exposed their homes to pollution.

Riding high
Early bicycles were known as 'boneshakers' and were only for the young and fit. They were also much too expensive for general use.

Housing for workers

Smoking chimneys day and night

Cotton mill

Chapel

Factory

Smoke from railway

Coal heap creates dust

Horse droppings fouled roads

Goods train

245

DEVELOPING ENTERTAINMENT

Culture for consumers

As the Industrial Revolution made countries richer, people began to have more money to spend on themselves – creating a demand for mass-produced art and entertainment. The results included cheaply produced books, sheet music and cheap musical instruments, as well as ornaments and pictures to decorate the home. Outside the home the entertainment included beer houses and gin shops, boxing booths, freak shows, travelling menageries and downmarket music halls offering sing-songs, jugglers and short, silly plays about lovers or murderers.

Art and advertising

As printing improved, advertisers could employ more skilled artists to create posters and packaging. Bubbles, used to sell Pears Soap, was painted by Sir John Everett Millais, the President of the Royal Academy.

William Morris

In reaction to cheap, ugly machine-made goods, William Morris (1834–1896) tried to revive the skills of the medieval craftsmen who created beautiful things regardless of profit. Morris' firm made stained glass and furniture for churches, and wallpaper, curtains and furniture for the home. Morris was also famous as a poet and an expert on eastern carpets. He campaigned to protect ancient buildings and in his old age revived the art of printing beautiful books.

Travelling circus
The first circus was created by Philip Astley in London in 1768. As roads improved, by around 1830 there were a growing number of travelling circuses.

In the ring
A typical circus combined displays of horsemanship with tumblers, jugglers and wild animals such as elephants. After around 1850, circuses featured trapeze acts, clowns and lion-tamers as popular ringside acts.

INDUSTRIAL FARMING

Mechanized farming

By the mid-19th century steam-powered machinery was being used by the wealthier farmers in Europe and America. Industry also supplied cheap iron tools, clay pipes to drain heavy soils and tiles to replace thatch on roofs.

Steam-powered farming
Linked up to the threshing machine, the steam engine could complete the job in a fraction of the time it used to take. Farming was becoming more intensive.

Horsepower
Horses still provided the main driving power on farms. Even the power of new engineering such as steam engines was measured in units of horsepower!

Mixed farming

Many farms both produced crops and raised livestock, rather than specializing in either. This was less risky than relying on a single product that could be wiped out by drought or disease.

Machine workers

While farmers prospered, their labourers rarely did. Harvest time meant very long hours, but in winter there was often little work, so little pay. As labourers left the land for better jobs in factories or to emigrate overseas, farmers brought in machines to do more work with fewer men.

Sheepshearing

Many farmers had huge flocks of sheep. The wool from their fleeces was always in demand.

TAYLOR

249

Efficient techniques

The first iron bridge in the world was built at Ironbridge, Shropshire in 1779. During the Industrial Revolution, mass-produced iron became cheap enough to use for building, but the industry was slow to adopt machinery and new construction methods. Early canals and railways were built using horses and men to shift tonnes of earth and stone. Steam power did aid big projects later, like building bridges, by driving cranes and pile-drivers. Railways meant bricks, slates and timber could be carried long distances cheaply.

Crystal Palace
This building was constructed of standardized iron sections in just four months, even though it was over 600 m in length. It was built to house the Great Exhibition of 1851 in London's Hyde Park.

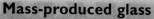

Mass-produced glass

Crystal Palace needed 294,000 glass panes. Each one was made at exactly the same size, making them much cheaper to produce than if they had been different sizes.

Temporary structures

After the Great Exhibition, Crystal Palace was taken down and rebuilt in southeast London for use as a leisure centre. During the Crimean War of 1854–1856, the British engineer Isambard Kingdom Brunel designed a prefabricated hospital ward that could easily be put up near a battlefield. Some architects today are deliberately designing buildings, such as London's Millennium Dome, to have a limited lifespan.

Eiffel Tower
Named after its designer, Gustav Eiffel, it was built in 1889 to commemorate the World's fair held to mark the centenary of the French Revolution. It was meant to last only 20 years.

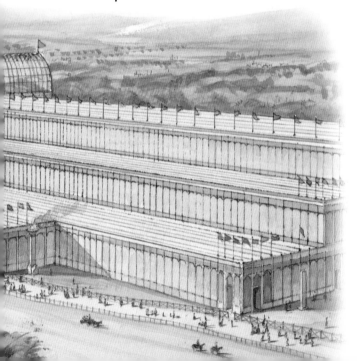

Chicago skyscrapers
The construction methods pioneered by Crystal Palace were later used to build the first skyscrapers in Chicago and New York in the 1880s and 1890s.

251

MEDICAL RESEARCH

Fighting infection

By the 18th century it was known that giving people a mild dose of smallpox, by scratching their skin and deliberately infecting them with it, could make them safe from it in later life. This was known as inoculation. The problem was to ensure the dose was a weak one. In 1796 the English doctor, Edward Jenner, discovered that a mild dose of cowpox gave protection with much less risk.

'King Cholera'

Cholera from India reached Britain in 1831, killing 50,000. Only much later was it understood that it was spread by infected water supplies. The answer was better sanitation.

Saving lives

Edward Jenner was a village doctor in Gloucestershire, England. His discovery made him famous but not rich because he gave away his secret and preferred to live quietly. Jenner's discovery was called 'vaccination' from the Latin for cow (vacca). The use of vaccinations spread quickly, saving millions of lives.

Germer killer

Pasteur had the idea that diseases were caused by germs. Lister applied the theory to surgery, using an antiseptic chemical spray to kill germs and so fight infection.

Research for cures

Progress in science began to provide doctors with more effective treatments throughout the 19th century. French scientist Louis Pasteur developed vaccines to treat deadly diseases such as rabies and anthrax. English doctor Joseph Lister used germ-killing antiseptics to halve the death rate from infections after surgery. Anaesthetics were used to end the agony of surgery.

The Curies

In 1903 Marie and Pierre Curie were awarded the Nobel Prize for discovering radium, which can cause and cure cancer. She died of radiation poisoning. Her notebooks are still too radioactive to be handled safely.

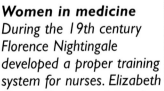

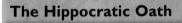

The Hippocratic Oath

Thomas Wakley founded the medical journal *The Lancet* to set standards and expose frauds who set themselves up as doctors. These fakes went against the principles of the Hippocratic Oath by putting their patients lives at risk through incompetence.

Women in medicine

During the 19th century Florence Nightingale developed a proper training system for nurses. Elizabeth Garrett Anderson (above) qualified as Britain's first woman doctor in 1865 after being refused training by three universities. The dispensary she founded in 1866 is now a women's hospital named after her.

ENGLISH LANGUAGE

The spread of English

The growth of Britain's trade and powerful empire made English the global language of commerce and learning. During the 19th century English overtook French as the language of international politics. English has the great advantage of being a language that is quite easy to learn – at least enough to be understood. It is now the world's most widely spoken second language and it is the standard language of aviation, science, medicine and computing.

North America

Pacific Ocean

Shakespeare
One of the most celebrated writers ever is the English playwright and poet William Shakespeare (1564–1616). He wrote 37 plays, including tragedies, comedies and historical dramas.

School for success
In the 19th century, American immigrants from all nations were eager for their children to learn English at school in order to succeed in life.

254

England

Europe

Asia

Atlantic
Ocean

Africa

Pacific
Ocean

South
America

Indian
Ocean

Oceania

Charles Dickens
*As a novelist, Dickens
(1813–1870) became
rich and famous on
both sides of the
Atlantic. Since his
death, his characters
have been reborn
many times through
films, radio and TV.*

Key to map

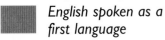
English spoken as a
first language

English used as a
government language

English spoken
among traders

Language of order and business

English became the main spoken language of the British Isles,
North America, the Caribbean and Oceania, as shown on the
map (above). Through the growth of the British Empire, it
became the language of government throughout much of Asia
and Africa, and was widely understood by traders in non-English
speaking areas like South America, coastal China and the
Persian Gulf.

SPORT

The spread of sport

As the British Empire spread, the British took their sports with them. The army encouraged sports such as boxing, riding and shooting competitions to keep soldiers occupied and fit. In India, army officers developed a local game to invent modern polo. British engineers building railways through remote areas filled in their leisure hours with cricket or soccer. Wherever migrants from Britain founded cities they would usually build a racetrack, and later on, tennis courts. American missionaries took baseball to Japan and British merchants introduced golf. Skiing developed as a sport in Norway and became known in California by the 1860s.

No swords
British sailors brought judo back from Japan with them. It had been invented as a form of unarmed self-defence during a time when the samurai, the elite Japanese warrior class, were the only people allowed to carry swords.

Importing ideas
The British introduced cricket to India during colonization. It is now the national sport of India, Pakistan, Sri Lanka and Bangladesh.

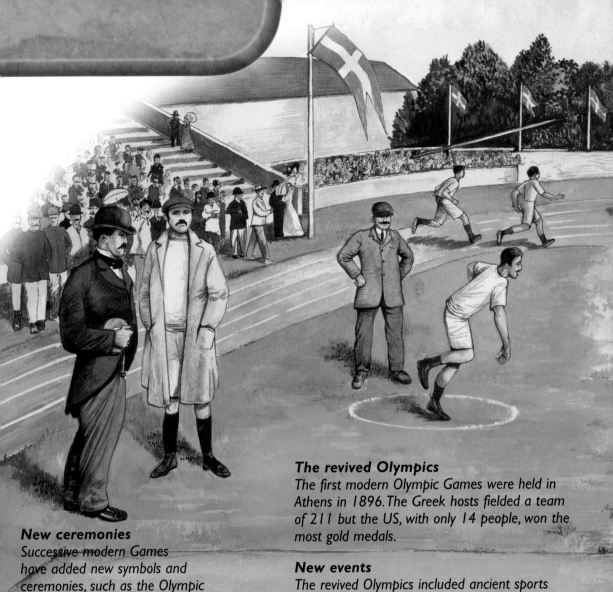

New ceremonies
Successive modern Games have added new symbols and ceremonies, such as the Olympic oath, flag and flame. The five rings on the Olympic flag represent the five continents of the world.

The revived Olympics
The first modern Olympic Games were held in Athens in 1896. The Greek hosts fielded a team of 211 but the US, with only 14 people, won the most gold medals.

New events
The revived Olympics included ancient sports such as wrestling, running and throwing the javelin. There were also new events such as shooting, fencing and cycling.

Goods for export

The spread of railways and steamships around the world made it possible to develop plantations, which grew a single crop on a large scale to be sold to buyers far away. Caribbean islands specialized in sugar, which was also made into rum and molasses. The American South produced cotton, tobacco, rice and indigo. Tea and coffee were grown in the British colonies of India, Sri Lanka and Kenya for export. Farming had entered the era of globalization.

Black and white

On American plantations the black slaves lived in wooden shacks, while the white owners lived in fine mansions. The division between rich white people and poor black people went on after slavery ended.

Self-sufficiency
Many plantations grew much of their own food and had their own carpenters and blacksmiths to make or repair tools, wagons, buildings and furniture.

Demand for rubber
Rubber was originally tapped from trees growing wild in the Amazon forests of Brazil. Rubber plants were later taken to Malaya (Malaysia), where they are not naturally found. By laying out plantations, with plants in neat rows, it was possible to collect rubber far more efficiently than from plants growing scattered at random. Demand for rubber grew rapidly from the 1880s with the coming of bicycles and cars needing tyres, and electrical goods needing insulation.

WARFARE DEVELOPMENT

Mass destruction

The history of warfare is the history of increasing firepower. In the American Civil War officers used revolvers, which could fire five or six shots before they had to be reloaded. Single-shot muskets gave way to repeating rifles and machine guns. In the 20th century the invention of planes brought aerial bombing, which could destroy whole cities, killing and injuring civilians as well as enemy soldiers.

Treating casualties

Since the Korean War (1950–1953) helicopters have been taking the wounded from the battlefield to frontline surgery. In the past, severe wounds had often meant death from loss of blood, shock or cold.

World War I trenches

On the command of the whistle blast, soldiers left their trench to advance towards enemy trenches. Few of the attackers survived.

Floating airbase

During World War II massive battles were fought between the US and Japanese navies in which the ships never saw each other but attacked using planes. Large-scale warfare has come to involve less face-to-face combat.

At the press of a button

The age of nuclear warfare began in August 1945 with the dropping of a single atomic bomb on the Japanese city of Hiroshima and another on Nagasaki. Both cities were flattened and about 100,000 people in each city were killed instantly. Radiation sickness killed many more over following years. Today's nuclear weapons are hundreds of times more powerful and can be launched from submarines thousands of kilometres from their target.

Breaking codes

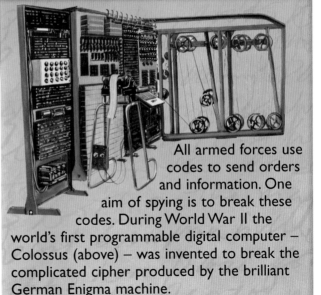

All armed forces use codes to send orders and information. One aim of spying is to break these codes. During World War II the world's first programmable digital computer – Colossus (above) – was invented to break the complicated cipher produced by the brilliant German Enigma machine.

GLOBALIZATION

Bullet Train

The world's first Bullet Train ran between the cities of Tokyo and Kyoto when Japan hosted the Olympics in 1964. It travelled at an average speed of 210 km/h and was a symbol of Japan's technological advances.

Global trade

By 1900 international trade had been revolutionized by fuel-efficient, steel-hulled steamships. Bulky goods, such as timber could be carried cheaply over thousands of kilometres. The invention of refrigerator ships made it possible to bring meat half-way round the world from New Zealand to Britain. Aircraft travel was at first so expensive it could only be used for passengers and mail but nowadays is used even for fruit and flowers. The use of computer technology has led to globalization. The world is now a marketplace where information is traded as much as things.

Stock market
Dealers in stocks and shares, currencies and commodities used to work face-to-face. Nowadays most dealing is done on screens using information technology.

Global travel

The Wright brothers' first flight was less than the length of a jumbo jet. In 1909 Frenchman Louis Bleriot flew across the English Channel. In 1927 American Charles Lindbergh flew 4830 km across the Atlantic alone. In 1961 Russian cosmonaut Yuri Gagarin became the first man to travel in space. US astronauts reached the Moon in 1969. Travel for ordinary people was revolutionized by cheap cars from the 1920s and cheap jet flights from the 1960s.

Passenger flight
A jumbo jet such as the Boeing 747 carries over 400 passengers. By making long-haul flights cheaper, jumbo jets opened up Asia and Africa to tourism.

Travel in the future
Reusable US space shuttles point the way to interplanetary travel. Planes may have reached their technological limit with Concorde, which was taken out of service in 2003. New airbus designs stress larger passenger loads, greater passenger safety, more efficient use of fuels, less noise and less pollution. Travel by air is now often cheaper than travel by land.

First plane flight
The first manned, powered flights were made by Orville and Wilbur Wright at Kittyhawk, North Carolina in 1903. The very first flight lasted just 12 seconds.

THE MODERN CITY

Instant communication
In the past, messenger-boys and postmen delivered information by hand. Computers, cables and satellites now link homes with each other and with massive stores of information via the Internet.

Cleaner living
Air pollution in cities now comes from vehicles rather than factories. As people move towards a cleaner environment we can expect a trend towards more pedestrian areas and bicycle lanes. In a world concerned with quality of life, people now demand that their towns be pleasant places in which to live.

Dotcom city
As steam power died out, the typical industrial town was transformed. Jobs increasingly depended on communicating information, rather than making things. Many people now commute to an office but others are using computer technology to work at home. The home-workshop lifestyle of the days before the Industrial Revolution is being reinvented. Concern for conservation means that old and new buildings can exist side-by-side. Even modern steel frame buildings have designs influenced by classical architecture.

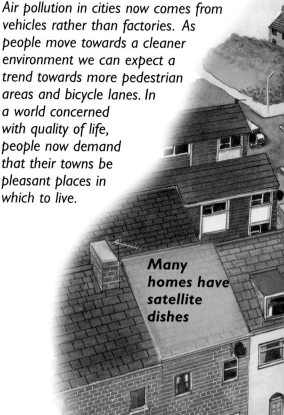

Many homes have satellite dishes

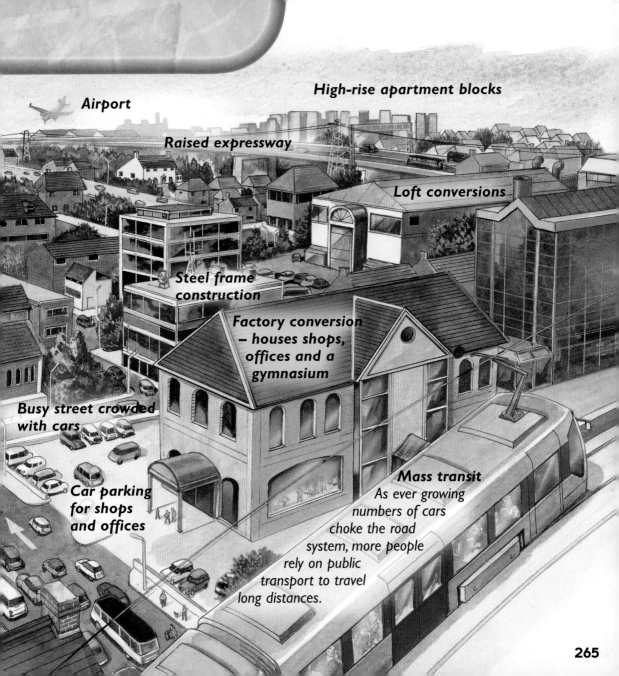

Airport

High-rise apartment blocks

Raised expressway

Loft conversions

Steel frame construction

Factory conversion – houses shops, offices and a gymnasium

Busy street crowded with cars

Car parking for shops and offices

Mass transit
As ever growing numbers of cars choke the road system, more people rely on public transport to travel long distances.

POWER AND INFLUENCE

Dictators and democrats

The history of the 20th century was dominated by struggles between democracies and dictatorships. Democracies such as the USA and Britain have governments that can be changed by free elections. In a dictatorship there is usually only one political party – and power is controlled by its leader. The dictatorships that took over much of Europe in the 20th century have now been replaced by democracies. Some, such as Denmark, Spain and Britain have an elected politician to run the country and a monarch for public ceremonies.

President Roosevelt

Franklin Delano Roosevelt (1882–1945) is the only person to have served as President of the United States four times. He is most famous for his policy called 'The New Deal', which led America out of the Great Depression in the 1930s.

Nelson Mandela
A fierce campaigner against South Africa's apartheid policies, Mandela spent 27 years in prison. In 1993 he won the Nobel Peace Prize. In 1994 he was elected President of South Africa in the country's first full democratic elections.

Lenin and Stalin
Vladimir Lenin (1870–1924, left) created the USSR as a Communist state. Joseph Stalin (1879–1953, right) ruled it as a brutal dictator. Both claimed to be building an ideal country for working people.

Changing faces
There have been four different portraits of the Queen shown on British coins since she took to the throne in 1953.

German dictator
Adolf Hitler (1889–1945) came to power in Germany in 1933. His followers treated him as a political and military genius. His attempt to conquer Europe led to Germany's disastrous defeat in World War II. In the end, Hitler shot himself and Germany was divided into two countries for the next fifty years.

267

World War I
World War I was the first war in which aircraft fought one another, and dropped bombs on the ground. The best dogfighter pilot was Germany's 'Red Baron'.

Tutankhamun
The tomb of Egyptian boy-king Tutankhamun was discovered in Egypt's Valley of the Kings in 1922. Although it had been robbed twice, the tomb was still intact. Tutankhamun's death mask was found inside the burial chamber.

Stonehenge
Stonehenge in England was built between 2950 and 1600 BC. The biggest stones are 9 m in length and weigh 50 tonnes — some came from a quarry 385 km away. It may have been built as a temple, a meeting place or an astronomical observatory.

Moon walk

American Neil Armstrong (left) was the first person on the Moon. He took a "giant leap for Mankind" on July 20 1969. *Apollo 11*'s other crew members were Edwin 'Buzz' Aldrin (right) and Michael Collins (centre).

Pyramids at Giza

The three enormous, four-sided pyramids at Giza in Egypt were built as tombs for Egypt's kings about 4500 years ago. They were the biggest, and are the only surviving element of the Seven Wonders of the Ancient World.

Great Wall of China

The Great Wall of China is the longest structure ever built by humans. Completed in the 200s BC to defend China from northern invaders, the Great Wall winds for over 6400 km. Thousands of people died while building it, which is why it came to be called the longest cemetery in the world.

AMAZING FACTS AND FIGURES

Julius Caesar

MOST FAMOUS ROMANS

Julius Caesar	General, almost became emperor but was murdered
Augustus	First emperor and winner of civil wars
Mark Antony	Soldier, fell in love with Cleopatra, Queen of Egypt
Hadrian	Emperor, famous for his wall in northern Britain
Constantine	First Christian emperor, AD 324–337

Mahatma Gandhi

NATIONAL HEROES

Joan of Arc	France
George Washington	United States
Simon Bolivar	Bolivia
Giuseppe Garibaldi	Italy
Nelson Mandela	South Africa
Martin Luther King	United States
Mahatma Gandhi	India
Horatio Nelson	Britain
William Tell	Switzerland
William Wallace	Scotland

Hanging Gardens

DID YOU KNOW?

The remains of Çatal Hüyük, an 8000-year-old town, were found in 1958 beneath a grass-covered mound in Turkey. About 5000 people lived there.

THE SIX LOST WONDERS OF THE ANCIENT WORLD

Name	Place	Date built	Date destroyed
Temple of Artemis	Ephesus, Turkey	550 BC	Destroyed AD 262
Statue of Zeus	Olympia, Greece	435 BC	Unknown end
Lighthouse, or pharos	Alexandria, Egypt	283–246 BC	Collapsed AD 1300s
Colossus	Rhodes	About 210 BC	Fell in earthquake, 224 BC
Hanging Gardens	Babylon, Iraq	Late 500s BC	Unknown end
Mausoleum at Halicarnassus	Bodrum, Turkey	353 BC	Fragments remain

Note: the seventh wonder, the pyramids of Egypt, is still standing

OUR PLANET

From America and Europe to Africa and Asia, this section is bursting with amazing facts about our planet.

What happened to the Aral Sea?
What is the smallest country?
Who was first to reach the South Pole?

Read on to find the answers to these and many other fascinating questions.

OUR PLANET EXPLAINED

NORTH AMERICA

Fewer than one person in ten in the world lives in North America, yet it is the powerhouse of the world. The USA has the biggest economy on Earth. America's mineral-rich northern neighbour, Canada, is one of the most prosperous countries in the world.

CENTRAL & SOUTH AMERICA

The mountains, jungles and plains of much of Central and South America have relatively few people. However, the coasts and river valleys of the Spanish- and Portuguese-speaking countries of Latin America are home to fast-expanding cities and a rapidly-growing population.

NORTHERN EUROPE

A small region, Northern Europe has influence throughout the world. A good climate and plentiful natural resources encouraged human settlement and development. Modern industry began in Northern Europe and today standards of living are among the highest in the world.

SOUTHERN EUROPE

The coastline of the Mediterranean Sea is cut into by deep bays and dotted with islands. Along its shores, the towns of Southern Europe are ancient and attractive. Once the birthplace of great civilisations, it is now one of the world's most popular regions for tourists.

NORTHERN ASIA

Northern Asia is an area of great contrasts and it supports nearly one-quarter of the world's people. It contains China, the country with the largest population, and some of the greatest industrial nations of the world, such as Japan and Korea.

SOUTHERN ASIA

Southern Asia is also home to over one-quarter of the world's population. The majority of the people who live in Southern Asia are involved in farming. The region also has huge cities and some of the most rapidly growing industries in the world.

NORTH AFRICA & THE MIDDLE EAST

Some of the world's oldest civilisations began in the river valleys of North Africa and the Middle East. Christianity and Islam also began in this region. Until the discovery of oil and natural gas in the 20th century, this region was relatively poor and undeveloped .

CENTRAL & SOUTHERN AFRICA

In the last century, Central and Southern Africa have probably seen more changes than any other part of the Earth. This is a region of new countries, with cities and industries where once there was none. However, this is also a region facing great problems – poverty, disease and wars.

OCEANIA

The Pacific Ocean occupies one-third of the Earth's surface. Across its waters are many islands – several large ones (Australia, New Guinea and the two main islands of New Zealand) and thousands of tiny islands. Together these lands form the continent of Oceania.

POLAR REGIONS

The polar regions are empty lands – too cold for many people to want to live there and too cold for farming. Yet under the ice and snow are natural riches – oil, natural gas, coal and metals – that may, one day, attract people when the world's natural resources run low.

FINDING RESOURCES

Bingham Canyon copper mine
Canada and the US have some the world's biggest concentrations of valuable minerals – coal, oil, iron ore, bauxite, copper, silver and zinc. Some minerals, such as copper, are mined in pits such as the massive copper mine at Bingham Canyon, near Salt Lake City (left).

A wealth of resources

The USA is self-sufficient in most minerals apart from oil and a few metals. The largest American oilfield is now in the Gulf of Mexico, off the coast of Texas, where there are drills and rigs at sea. The most potential in the US is in northern Alaska where large deposits of oil and natural gas have been found. However, extracting oil in cold conditions would present extra problems.

Vital mineral
Oil is the most valuable mineral resource in Texas – the state produces about one quarter of the United States' oil.

Overfishing

The mixing of currents in the shallow seas off eastern Canada produces the ideal conditions for the tiny creatures that are the main food of vast shoals of fish. But too many fish have been taken and now there are not enough to reproduce and replace stocks. As a result many small Canadian fishing ports have had to stop fishing.

Preserving the catch
In the small ports of Newfoundland, Canada, fish used to be hung out to dry to preserve it. Now almost all of the catch is frozen on the fishing ships.

Alaskan oil pipeline
Oil has to be brought long distances by pipeline to where it is needed. To bring oil from northern Alaska has involved building through protected areas and national parks.

AMERICAN WONDERS

Pioneers of leisure

America 'invented' the modern leisure park such as Disneyworld, Disneyland and Epcot. More than half of all Americans visit an amusement park at least once a year. The USA also pioneered the idea of the national park – an area of natural beauty protected from development. Among the most visited is the Golden Gate National Park. Spectacular landscapes are also a draw for visitors, such as the Grand Canyon or Niagara Falls.

Famous bridge
The Golden Gate National Park is home to the bridge of the same name, which is one of the longest suspension bridges in the world.

International waterfall
Niagara Falls consists of two waterfalls – the American Falls in the United States and the Horseshoe Falls in Canada. The Niagara river forms a natural border between the two countries.

Appetite for height

The tallest structure in the world is the CN Tower in Toronto, Canada. At 555 m in height, the 130,000-tonne concrete tower is topped by a revolving restaurant. On a clear day, it is possible to see hills 120 km away.

Gateway to the west

The 'Wild West' is an attraction both for its scenery and history. The so-called 'gateway to the West' is the city of St Louis, which now has a real gateway – a steel-covered arch measuring 192 m in height.

Grand Canyon

The Grand Canyon in Arizona has been carved out by the Colorado River. It is 446 km long, 1.6 km deep, and is 1–29 km wide. The Canyon is now part of a national park.

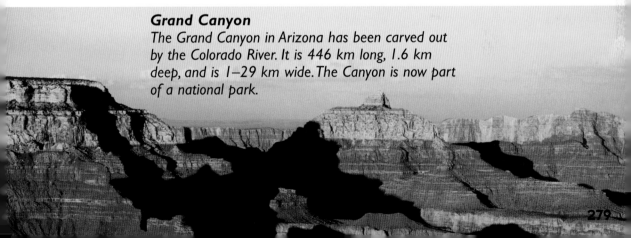

TECTONIC PLATES

Earthmoving

The outer layer of our planet (the crust) is divided into about 15 sections called 'tectonic plates'. These plates 'float' on top of a molten layer beneath. Plates move very slowly – a few millimetres a year on average. Where these plates collide, the Earth's surface is compressed and buckles up to form mountains, known as 'fold' mountains. The Alps were formed by the African plate moving northwards into the Eurasian Plate. The Rocky Mountains formed where the Pacific Plate pressed against the North American Plate. The Rocky Mountains are still slowly rising as the pressure between the two plates continues. All the world's biggest mountain ranges are on the edges of plates.

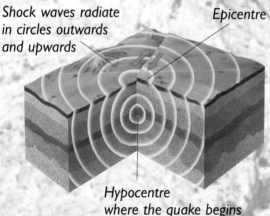

Shock waves radiate in circles outwards and upwards

Epicentre

Hypocentre where the quake begins

What makes the earth quake

The boundaries between plates (above) are often earthquake zones. In California, two plates are slowly sliding against one another along the San Andreas Fault. These plates can lock together for hundreds of years. The pressure builds up, then suddenly, the plates slip past each other to create a major earthquake.

Pop-up mountains

Not all mountains are fold mountains, formed where plates press against one another. Some mountain ranges – far away from the edges of plates – are the result of plates moving elsewhere. Pressure makes mountains 'pop up' between huge cracks (faults). Examples in the USA include the Black Hills of Dakota and the Adirondack Mountains of New York State.

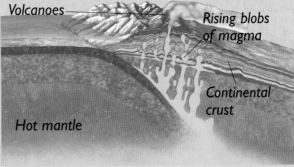

Volcanoes

Rising blobs of magma

Continental crust

Hot mantle

Jagged edge

The Rocky Mountains run down western North America for about 4800 km. They contain the highest peak in Canada (Mount Logan) and in the United States (Mount McKinley). They look jagged because water freezes in cracks and forces rocks to break apart.

Left standing

No matter how high a mountain, it will eventually be worn away by erosion. Rain washes away small grit. Rivers eat away valleys. Yet, in places, a layer of very hard rock will not be worn away so easily. This has happened in the American West where dramatic tall pillars, topped by hard rock, have been left standing, while softer material has been eroded away on either side.

US ECONOMY

A strong economy

The US is self-sufficient in most products. It has the raw materials for nearly everything it needs. Principal industries include iron and steel, motor vehicles, electronic engineering, food processing, chemicals, cement, aluminium, aerospace industries, telecommunications, textiles and clothing, and consumer goods. America's economy is half as big again as its nearest rival, Japan. The strength of that economy, and of its currency, the dollar, allows the US to dominate the world.

Wall Street

The United States has the largest economy of any nation on Earth. Wall Street (right), in New York City, is its financial centre, housing the world's biggest stock exchange and many banks.

Dotcom

The Internet developed in America. Many computing companies are based on the West Coast, Seattle or in 'Silicon Valley', California. The popularity of the Internet continues to grow. Many businesses are now Internet-based.

Mass production

In 1908, American Henry Ford introduced mass-production, the assembly-line factory. Cars could be made quickly and cheaply. The motor vehicle industry is one of the largest in North America.

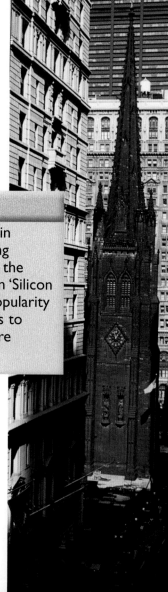

HOLLYWOOD

Shop, shop, shop!

Industry does not just mean making things. The biggest employer in the US now is service industries – shops, hotels, catering, leisure and finance. Service industries involve about three-quarters of the US labour force and one of the largest sections is shopping. America gave the modern shopping mall to the world.

The silver screen

In the early days of film, the sunlight of California attracted movie-makers who filmed largely outdoors. Hollywood, Los Angeles, became the world's film capital and later attracted television. However, Bombay in India actually makes more films.

RIVERS AND WATERFALLS

The life of a river

Rivers get their water from rainfall and melting snow. Most rivers are joined by other, smaller rivers along their course, called tributaries. The area draining into one river is called a drainage basin – the largest is the Amazon Basin in Brazil. A river carries mud, stones and plant remains that it has eroded and picked up from the ground it flows over. When it slows down near the sea this material is often deposited in the form of land, called a delta. The Amazon Delta is the largest in the world.

Lake in the clouds
At just over 3800 m above sea level, the world's highest navigable lake is Lake Titicaca in Bolivia. Local people use reed boats (above) for transport around the lake.

No rain terrain
In the north of Chile and southern Peru lies the Atacama Desert (right), the driest place on Earth. The Atacama is a desert because no moist air blows onto it from the adjoining ocean to fall as rain.

Water power

Rivers are 'harnessed' to generate electricity. Dams are constructed to hold back artificial lakes (reservoirs). Water is dropped from the top of the dam to turn turbines to produce electricity. One of the world's largest dams is the Itaipu Dam on the Paraná River where Paraguay meets Brazil.

Iguazú Falls

Where rivers reach a fault or an area of soft rock, they often tumble over it to form a waterfall. The Iguazú Falls, forming a natural border between Brazil and Argentina, is one of the world's largest waterfalls in terms of the amount of water that flows over it. Downstream is a 'lost' waterfall – the larger Guaira Falls, which were covered by a reservoir.

285

CENTRAL & SOUTH AMERICAN CITIES

A better life

The rapidly growing cities in this region are busy, polluted and crowded with slum housing. São Paolo, Buenos Aires and Rio de Janeiro, all in South America, are among the world's largest cities. Millions of people in Central and Southern America want to move north to the USA to improve their lives. America tries to keep out many of these immigrants – there are just not enough jobs and houses in the USA for them all.

Housing the poor

Bogota (below), the capital city of Colombia, and Rio de Janeiro (right) have many of the problems of the large cities of South America. These cities have grown so quickly that there is not enough housing. The city centres have stunning modern skyscrapers, but around the fringes there are poor shanty towns.

Illegal immigrants

Every year between 800,000 and 2 million people from Central and Southern America enter the US illegally. Most of these people ecome from Mexico. The US–Mexican border as strict controls to try to prevent this.

Tourist attractions

Mexico is a relatively short flight from the large cities of western USA. Resorts in Mexico offer a cheaper holiday for American tourists, as well as beautiful scenery and the attraction of being in another country. Acapulco was a small village 100 years ago, but is now a bustling seaside resort with more than half a million people.

Growing cities

The last 100 years has been a time when huge cities have grown. Farming has used more machinery and needed a smaller labour force, while industry in towns has increased, requiring more workers. In 1900, only 12 cities in the world had more than one million inhabitants. Now more than 300 cities house over one million people. Some of the biggest of these cities are in Central and South America.

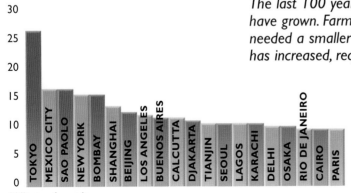

Millions of people

URBAN EXPANSION

Population explosion

Central and South America have seen an enormous population growth in the last 100 years – from just over 50 million in 1900 to more than 500 million by the year 2000. Cities have grown, industries have flourished and nearly half of the forests that once covered the region have been cut down. The result has been pollution on a huge scale, with poisoned rivers and slums surrounding the cities.

Unexplored regions

South America contains some of the world's last unexplored places. The Amazon Basin is still being explored for minerals. For this, roads and airstrips are built. This invasion destroys forests and threatens the way of life of tribes who live there, such as the Yanomami. They live uncomplicated lives, taking from the forest only what they need for food and shelter.

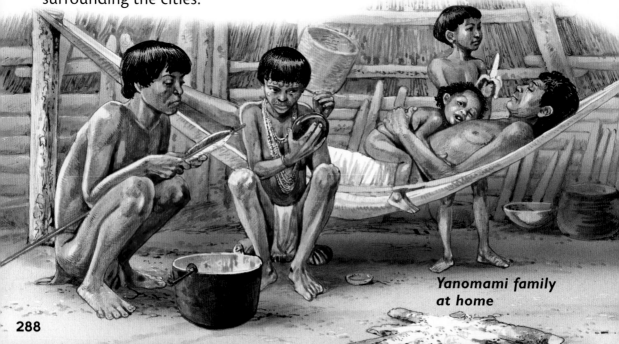

Yanomami family at home

Urban waste

The world is running out of places to put rubbish such as packaging. Recycling breaks down rubbish into raw materials to use again. In Mexico City, what the rich throw away as rubbish, the poor often retrieve from dumps to reuse.

Choking cities

Streets of the cities of Central and South America are filled with vehicles. Fumes from car exhaust gases pollute the air and are the main part of the smog that blankets some cities. Mexico City is particularly badly affected because its centre lies in a basin in which the smog becomes trapped.

Deforestation

The Amazon Basin contains the world's largest tropical rainforest. But every year an area about half the size of Scotland is cleared and then burned to make new farmland for Brazil's many landless peasants. Many plant and animal species lose their habitat and become extinct.

RANCH FARMING

Land of contrasts

Central and Southern America is a region of tropical jungles, sub-tropical forest, deserts, and mountains. However, in the south in Argentina, Uruguay and southern Brazil lies one of the world's great farming regions. Grasslands provide pasture for cattle in the pampas and for sheep in the cooler Patagonia. In the eastern hills and coastal regions of Brazil are farms that specialize in a single crop – usually either coffee or cocoa.

New discoveries

When Europeans rediscovered the Americas in the 1400s they not only found new lands, they discovered a range of new crops that were to change the lives of Europeans, including cocoa (from Mexico), maize (Mexico) and potatoes (Peru). The explorer Christopher Columbus discovered tobacco (right) in Cuba in 1492. Since then its cultivation has spread around the world.

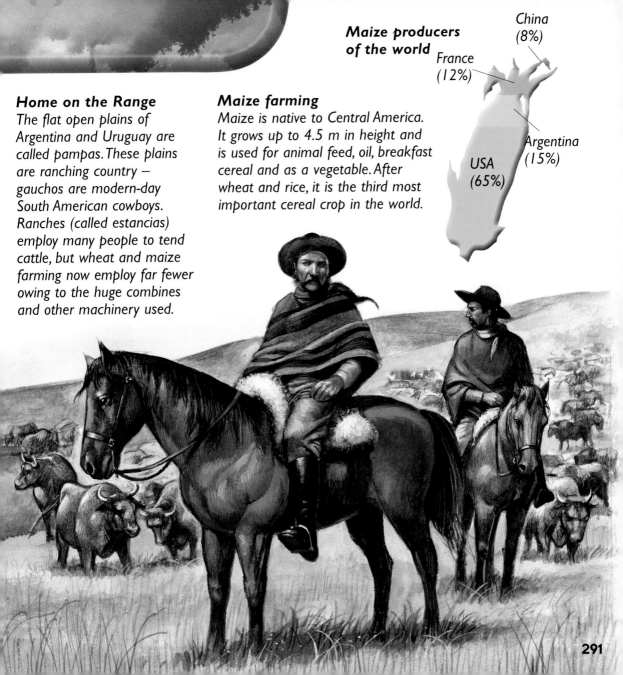

Maize producers of the world

China (8%)

France (12%)

Argentina (15%)

USA (65%)

Home on the Range

The flat open plains of Argentina and Uruguay are called pampas. These plains are ranching country – gauchos are modern-day South American cowboys. Ranches (called estancias) employ many people to tend cattle, but wheat and maize farming now employ far fewer owing to the huge combines and other machinery used.

Maize farming

Maize is native to Central America. It grows up to 4.5 m in height and is used for animal feed, oil, breakfast cereal and as a vegetable. After wheat and rice, it is the third most important cereal crop in the world.

Commuter culture

One quarter of the world's industries are concentrated in Northern Europe, which is a densely populated region. The southern part of the Netherlands (where many people are crammed into a small area), the Ruhr industrial area in Germany, London and Paris are overcrowded. People are living farther from their work. Good roads (for example German autobahns) and railway systems allow people to live in smaller towns and to travel into the big cities to work – this is called commuting.

Leisure time

A high standard of living – and a low age at which people retire from work – means that people in northern Europe have plenty of leisure time. In Belgium, Finland and France, for example, most people retire below the age of 60.

Channel Tunnel

It takes 20 minutes to travel from Britain to France by the Eurostar train through the Channel Tunnel. The tunnel is nearly 50 km in length – 37 km of this is underwater.

Percentages of Europeans living in the countryside

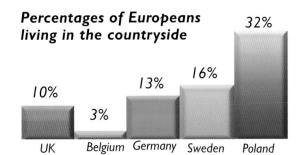

10%	3%	13%	16%	32%
UK	Belgium	Germany	Sweden	Poland

In Poland about a quarter of the nation's workforce is employed in agriculture. Many of the farms are small and worked on by the owners. The most important crops are sugar beet, potatoes and cereals.

Supermarkets

It is now unusual in Northern Europe to find many food shops in city centres. As most people have cars, giant supermarkets have been built in the outskirts of large towns.

Average national incomes

Luxembourg £33,100 (the highest in the world), Switzerland £27,800, Norway £27,600, Denmark £25,100, Sweden £21,900, Finland £21,500 and Germany £21,100.

NATURAL ENERGY

Natural power sources

The natural heat of the Earth can be used to produce power. In Iceland, where geysers shoot steam into the sky, water from hot springs is piped to heat all the buildings in the capital, Reykjavik. This hot water also warms greenhouses, which make Iceland almost self-sufficient in vegetables for salads. But there are very few places in the world like Iceland where natural heat from our planet can be used in this way.

Eruption of steam

Geysers occur when cold underground water reaches rocks that are hot. The water heats to form steam, which then erupts from the earth in a tall column.

Water power

Water power in Europe once meant water wheels built across small streams to power mills. In the 18th century the huge coal deposits of the continent began to be used and industries moved to coalfields. Now, water power is important again. In northern Europe many deep narrow valleys have been dammed. This dam is in Scotland, but Norway and Sweden are greater producers of electricity from dams.

Fossilization

Coal is a fossil. It is made from the remains of plants that lived millions of years ago. Fossils form where plant or animal remains laid down in rocks are gradually replaced with dissolved minerals over millions of years. In coal, the plant material has been crushed to form a hard deposit.

Drilling for oil

Oil rigs are built far out at sea in order to extract natural resources from the seabed, which are then refined to produce fuel. The rigs are tough structures made of steel and concrete. They can withstand huge waves and storms. Permanent rigs can sometimes support an ecosystem as their underwater structures form artificial reefs.

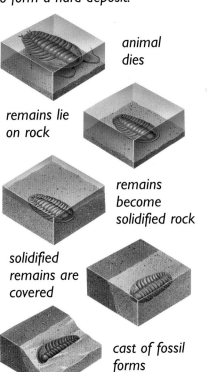

animal dies

remains lie on rock

remains become solidified rock

solidified remains are covered

cast of fossil forms

MODERN INDUSTRY

Computing
Modern computing, emails and the Internet, mean that many people are able to work at home. They can communicate electronically with other people who are working on the same project. Home working means that fewer people have to commute regularly into the big cities to offices.

Click!
Creating new designs have been made easy with new technology. A textile designer can create a repeat pattern with just a click of a mouse.

Under threat

Northern Europe was the world's first great industrial region. But it did not have all the raw materials it needed. European industry relied on trade (and in the past on trade with colonies). Today, Europe's industries are under threat from places where workers are cheaper. For example, much of Northern Europe's textile industry has disappeared unable to compete with Asia.

Coal mining

Modern industry began in Northern Europe at the end of the 18th century. Coal was used to power factories and Europe's great industrial areas developed on coalfields.

City of London

The city of London is the financial centre of Europe, with the continent's largest stock exchange and the headquarters of many banks. The reasons are historic. In the 19th century, Britain was the major economic and industrial power in Europe.

The largest port

The Dutch port of Rotterdam is the largest port in the world. It grew as the principal port for Europe's greatest industrial region, the Ruhr in north-west Germany.

COMMUNISM

European upheaval

Northern Europe has seen major changes in the past century. World Wars I and II were fought in Northern Europe from 1914–1918 and then 1939–1945. After the World War II, Russia (then known as the Soviet Union) set up Communist governments in Eastern Europe. But the Communist system did not work, and the countries ruled by the Communists fell further and further behind Western Europe. Between 1989 and 1991, these Communist governments collapsed.

Changes in Europe

During the 1900s, after World Wars I and II, Europe underwent huge political changes. A Communist government took control in Russia in 1917. This new Soviet Union came to dominate eastern countries. But in 1991 when the Soviet Union collapsed, more than ten countries gained the freedom to become independent.

Europe, 1914

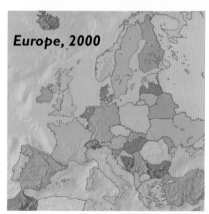

Europe, 2000

From east to west

Since the 'Iron Curtain' (a divide between the countries in eastern Europe and those in western Europe) came down, the people of eastern Europe have been free to move within the continent. Many thousands of people from the east and particularly from the poorer countries in south-eastern Europe such as Albania and Romania have moved to the richer countries of north-western Europe in search of better jobs, better homes and better lives. These people are known as 'economic refugees'. Their arrival in a new country, sometimes illegally, has caused problems and resentment even though there are jobs for them in Northern Europe.

Changing boundaries

Germany, divided in two since 1945, was reunited in 1990. The Soviet Union broke up into 15 countries as Russia's grip on the peoples it ruled loosened. Estonia, Latvia and Lithuania, among others, broke away from Russia to become independent European countries. Yugoslavia was split up in a series of wars.

The Berlin wall

For nearly 50 years Germany was split by a wall that stopped people fleeing to the west from the communist east. The wall physically divided the city of Berlin. When Communism eventually collapsed, the wall was torn down in 1990. Only small, ruined sections remain.

European Union

In the 1950s, the countries of western Europe formed a trading organization, now called the European Union. Since then this group has become closer and includes Austria, Belgium (whose capital Brussels, left, is the EU's headquarters), Denmark, Finland, France, Germany, Greece, Ireland, Italy, Luxembourg, the Netherlands, Portugal, Spain, Sweden and the UK.

THE MEDITERRANEAN CLIMATE

Autumn storms

Mediterranean winters can be wet, but often the greatest amount of rain in southern Europe comes in thunderstorms in the autumn, when spectacular lightning displays light the sky.

Angle of sunlight

The big seasonal difference in temperature is due to the movement of the Sun. When the Mediterranean is nearest to the Sun in midsummer, it is hottest and driest. The coolest time of year comes when the Sun is farthest away from the Mediterranean, and closer to the southern hemisphere.

Tropic of Cancer

Tropic of Capricorn

Microclimates

There are lots of local variations in the weather because of the many bays lining the Mediterranean coast, and the mountains surrounding it.

Climate types

Mountains

Temperate forest

Desert

Hot air and cold winds

Southern Europe – the area north of the Mediterranean Sea – has what is called a 'Mediterranean' climate. This type of climate has mild, wet winters and hot, dry summers. Some parts of the Mediterranean get extremely hot in summer. This heats up the air, which then rises. To take its place, cooler air rushes in from nearby. This causes the many strong local winds for which the Mediterranean is famous. One example is the Mistral, a cold dry wind that blows down the Rhône valley in France towards the Mediterranean. This lowers the temperature in late autumn and early winter.

Sun-soaked slopes
Winter rain is stored in reservoirs and tanks and is used in spring and summer to irrigate the fruit for which Southern Europe is famous. On sunny south-facing slopes, farmers have grown vines, olives, oranges and lemons for centuries.

Weather in Athens, Greece

Average temperature:
11°C – December
26°C – June

Average rainfall:
137 mm – December
18 mm – June

MEDITERRANEAN TRADITIONS

Walled towns

The old towns of the Mediterranean shores and inland were built on hills to avoid low-lying marshes where mosquitoes bred. In the Middle Ages, to avoid attacks by pirates, these towns were walled so that they could be easily defended. As a result these traditional towns were quite cramped with little room to spare for gardens. Streets are narrow and often steep.

Holy days

Living so close together, people tend to be sociable. Many towns have festivals, often when different parts of the town compete against each other. Festivals include bull running in Spain and horse races through streets in Italy.

Siesta

The working day begins early before it gets too hot and shops often close for several hours at midday. Many have an afternoon snooze – siesta – and then enjoy eating outdoors later.

Special days

Most of Southern Europe is Catholic. The Catholic Church has many special days, including saints' days when there are processions and other festivities where statues of saints are carried through streets. Although many do not actually go to church now, traditional religious festivals still play an important part in people's lives.

SOUTHERN EUROPEAN FARMING

A juicy industry

Orange groves are part of the Mediterranean scene. Each tree produces about 70 kg of oranges a year. Spain, Italy and Greece are among the world's highest producers.

Olives

The olive is grown for its tiny 'berry' crushed to make oil for cooking as well as to eat as a 'fruit'. The small trees are tolerant of different soils but do not like standing in wet soil, so the Mediterranean slopes are ideal.

Health and diet

Olive oil is an important part of Mediterranean cooking, which features fresh fruit and vegetables and plenty of fish. This healthy diet helps Southern Europeans live a long, healthy life.

Small farms

Southern Europe has a Mediterranean climate – hot, dry summer, and cooler winter with some rain. It is a region of many small farms, some with only a few hectares. Soils can be poor and rocky and the land is often steep. South-facing slopes can be used for olive groves and vineyards. Flatter areas, with better soil, are used for orange groves, lemon groves and a wide variety of vegetables. Some slopes are terraced.

Other (28%)

Italy (26%)

Spain (33%)

Greece (13%)

Olive producers of the world

Irrigation

Because rainfall is low – and in summer often almost non-existent – irrigation is important. Water from the autumn thunderstorms and winter rains is stored in tanks and reservoirs and piped to the fields in late spring and summer.

TOURIST ATTRACTIONS

Ruins in cities

Southern Europe was the birthplace of two great civilizations – the ancient Greeks and the Romans. Temples, aqueducts, walls, palaces and other ancient remains are found throughout the region. Nowhere are they more spectacular than Rome, in Italy, or Athens, in Greece. In central Rome is the forum, the marketplace of ancient Rome, surrounded by temples. Athens is overlooked by a hill town (the Acropolis) and its famous temple, the Parthenon.

Tourist attractions

Southern Europe is one of the major tourist regions of the world. People were first attracted in great numbers from northern Europe in the 1960s by cheap holidays in a region where dry sunny summer weather is almost guaranteed. Spain, where the tourism industry employs 1.5 million people, is the main destination, receiving 70 million visitors every year.

Ruined temple
The Parthenon was constructed from white marble to honour Athena, the goddess of Athens. All the sculptures that once covered it have been taken away or destroyed.

Style capital

Spain's second city, Barcelona, is one of the most stylish places in Europe. Among its famous buildings is the unfinished church of the Sagrada Familia (below). The city adjoins the bustling holiday resorts of the Costa Brava.

Smallest country

Vatican City, home of the Pope and headquarters of the Roman Catholic Church, is the smallest country in the world. Dominated by the dome of St Peter's Cathedral, Vatican City draws millions of Catholic pilgrims every year.

Istanbul

Istanbul is one of the main sights of Turkey, a country that attracts 10 million visitors a year. Some are drawn to the beaches, others to the low price of holidays – things are much cheaper than in Northern Europe. A string of ruined ancient Greek and Roman cities attracts visitors, as well as mosques such as the Hagia Sofia (right).

THE ARAL SEA

Shrinking sea

The Aral Sea, in Kazakhstan and Uzbekistan, was once the world's fourth largest lake. Now it is less than half the size it was 40 years ago. The reason for this is that water from the two main rivers feeding the lake has been diverted to irrigate the cotton fields of Uzbekistan, and for use in cities. Not enough water reaches the lake to maintain it. So, year by year, the lake grows smaller – 135 of the 173 species of animals and fish that used to live in the lake have now become extinct and the surrounding land is becoming desert.

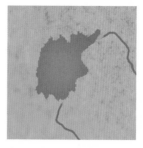 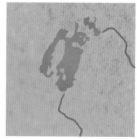

Aral Sea before and after
Compare the size and shape of the Aral Sea in the 1960s (left), when more river water flowed into it, and how it looks today (right) split in two and still shrinking.

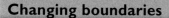
Changing boundaries

The countries of central northern Asia used to be ruled by Russia as part of the Soviet Union. But in 1991 the Soviet Union broke up into 15 independent countries. One of these new countries, Kazakhstan, the tenth largest country in the world in area, faces major problems of pollution from old factories.

308

Stranded ships

Because the Aral Sea has shrunk, ports that were once on the lake shore are now 65 km from the water's edge. Ships lie marooned in the desert where once there were fishing grounds.

Space to live and work

Japan is a very overcrowded country. Most of its 127 million inhabitants live in the small areas of lowland along Japan's southern coasts. There is great demand for this flat land, for housing and industries like Japan's car factories, which make one in five of the world's cars. These factories spread over what could otherwise be valuable farming land.

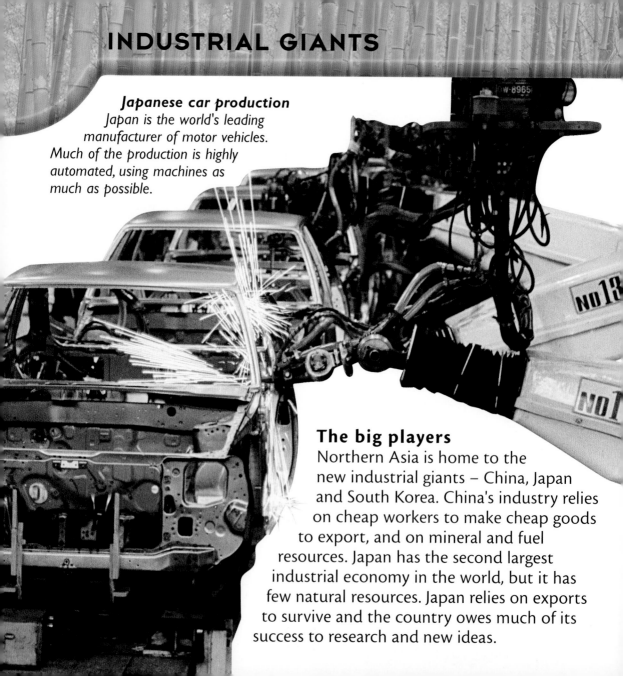

INDUSTRIAL GIANTS

Japanese car production
Japan is the world's leading manufacturer of motor vehicles. Much of the production is highly automated, using machines as much as possible.

The big players
Northern Asia is home to the new industrial giants – China, Japan and South Korea. China's industry relies on cheap workers to make cheap goods to export, and on mineral and fuel resources. Japan has the second largest industrial economy in the world, but it has few natural resources. Japan relies on exports to survive and the country owes much of its success to research and new ideas.

Growing finance

The growth of industry has led to the development of major banks and stock exchanges in the region. The stock exchanges at Tokyo and Hong Kong are among the five largest in the world. China did not have any stock exchanges a generation ago, but now has four, including one at Shenzhen, a boom city near Hong Kong. Shenzhen has grown from a fishing village to a city with over one million inhabitants in 25 years.

Quality goods

The electrical goods industries of Northern Asia began by making cheap goods, for example in the island of Taiwan. In the 1980s and 1990s, the countries of this region started to specialize more in quality items. Japan, China and South Korea now lead the world in the production of electronic equipment and electrical goods.

Shanghai trade centre

China's largest city, Shanghai, is also the headquarters of many of the country's largest companies and the home of the main Chinese stock exchange. All along China's eastern and southern coasts, industry is flourishing and cities expanding. In Shanghai's case, the city is growing rapidly both outwards and upwards. Two of the world's highest office buildings are under construction in Shanghai and a whole new business district is being built.

ANCIENT ATTRACTIONS

Ancient sites

Northern Asia is a region full of amazing ancient ruins and monuments, such as the famous 'army' of terracotta soldiers at Xian, in China. There is also breathtaking scenery such as the unique, pointy limestone peaks of southern China, or the icy wastes of Siberia in Russia. There may be much to see but taking holidays is a recent development in Northern Asia. In Japan, South Korea and parts of China, people are now becoming wealthy and have money to spend on travel. However, people take little leisure time and fewer holidays than is common in the West.

Tourists welcome

China is opening up to tourism. Twenty years ago, the Chinese government discouraged visitors. Now, nearly ten million foreign tourists come to China every year. One of the main attractions in Beijing, the capital, is the Forbidden City, a vast complex of temples and palaces that was the home of Chinese emperors for centuries.

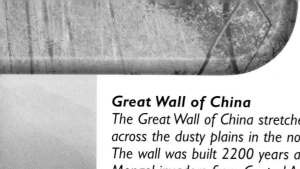

Great Wall of China

The Great Wall of China stretches for 3460 km across the dusty plains in the north of the country. The wall was built 2200 years ago to keep out Mongol invaders from Central Asia. The wall varies between 5–16 m in height and has a defensive tower positioned about every 60 m.

Modern attractions

Not all of the famous buildings and sights of Northern Asia are ancient. China is now building some of the tallest skyscrapers in the world. Few cities have as many spectacular modern buildings as Hong Kong (right), which was once a British colony. Hong Kong is a major port, and business and manufacturing centre.

Japanese sights

Japan attracts relatively few foreign tourists – it is a long way from North America and Western Europe, where most of the world's tourists come from. The snow-capped volcano Mount Fuji and the ancient remains at Kyoto (left) are popular places for Japanese tourists to visit.

WEALTH AND POVERTY

Japanese village
Although 78 percent of Japanese people live in towns and cities, the warmer climate of the islands of Kyushi and Shikoki allows farming communities to thrive.

Rich and poor
This region contains some of the most exciting, rapidly growing modern cities in the world – Shanghai, Tokyo, Seoul and Hong Kong. It also includes areas that are remote and poor, even within the same countries. Far western and north-western China is poor, while the cities of the south and east coasts of China have a high standard of living. And deep in Central Asia, countries such as Uzbekistan and Tajikistan are very poor.

Hong Kong
Hong Kong has a standard of living almost as high as that of Northern European countries. Many people think the 21st century will be the 'Pacific Century', with the greatest increases in prosperity being along the Asian edge of the Pacific Ocean – in places such as Hong Kong.

Scientists have proved a link between what we eat and our health. In Northern Asia, people eat more fish and vegetables. This healthy, low fat diet has helped the Japanese to become one of the longest-lived nation on Earth.

Traffic jams

Cities in Asia have grown so quickly that the transport has not had time to catch up. Most North Asian cities suffer from traffic gridlock – and where many cannot afford a car, bicycle jams are common.

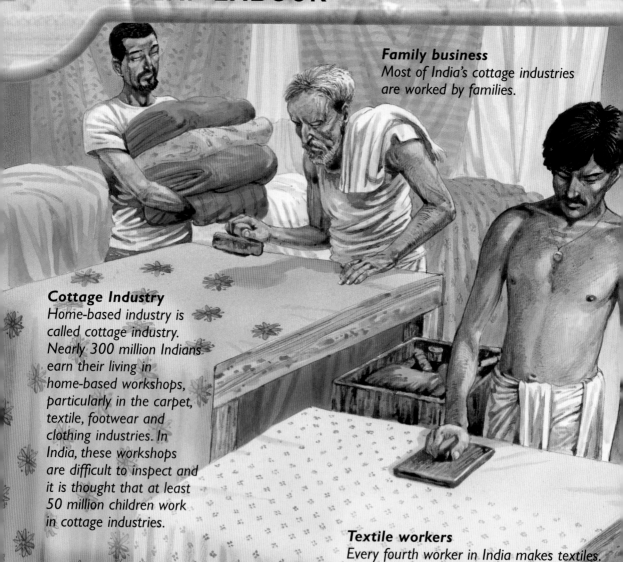

CHEAP LABOUR

Family business
Most of India's cottage industries are worked by families.

Cottage Industry
Home-based industry is called cottage industry. Nearly 300 million Indians earn their living in home-based workshops, particularly in the carpet, textile, footwear and clothing industries. In India, these workshops are difficult to inspect and it is thought that at least 50 million children work in cottage industries.

Textile workers
Every fourth worker in India makes textiles. Textiles are used to make clothes for export and for sale to tourists.

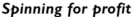
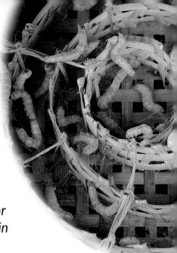

Petronas Towers
Standing at 492 m in height, the 88-storey Petronas Towers dominate the skyline of the capital of Malaysia, Kuala Lumpur. The towers have become a symbol of Malaysia's economic growth.

Spinning for profit
Silk is obtained from the webs spun by silkworms. Keeping silk worms has been a traditional activity in some cooler parts of Southern Asia. The region is now important for the production of artificial silk in factories using cheap labour.

'Tiger Economies'

Industry in much of South Asia is traditionally small scale and requiring lots of workers rather than machinery. This is the case in India and Pakistan where there is not the demand for so many modern goods – many people cannot afford them. Over one-third of India's population lives below the official poverty line. Other countries such as Thailand and Malaysia have been so successful that they are called 'tiger economies'. Big companies from Japan and Taiwan have invested in these countries, setting up factories to make inexpensive parts for their industries.

Dotcom
Some South Asian countries have adopted the Internet and modern computer technology eagerly. Singapore, for example, aims to put every citizen on the Internet. At least 90 percent of the population has now been connected.

317

RICH PRODUCE

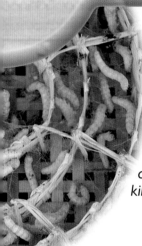

Silk worm farms
Most of the world's silk is produced in Asia. Silk worms spin a cocoon, each of which contains more than 700 m of thread. But it takes 6 kg of cocoons to make one kilogram of silk.

A rice diet
Southern Asia is one of the most densely populated regions on Earth. Many of the people rely upon one crop – rice. In fact, more than half of the world's population depends upon rice for food. Of the seven main producers of rice in the world, six are in Southern Asia. Scientists have worked to produce better varieties of rice that yield more grain. Since the 1960s the yield of some rice plants has increased by 700 percent.

Tea picking
Tea is grown in the cooler hills of India and Sri Lanka. Many people work on tea plantations, picking the leaves from the tea bushes. Many of the workers are women.

Tea clipper
In the 1700s and 1800s, ships – tea clippers – brought tea to Britain from India. Foreign money was needed to develop tea plantations. It takes four years before a tea bush will produce leaves for tea.

Rice terraces

Cutting terraces in hillsides allows farmers to grow crops on land that would otherwise be inaccessible. Terraces are edged with walls, normally built of stone, to hold back water to create the flooded conditions rice needs to grow.

Rice harvesting

Farming for rice is hard work. It is planted by hand, harvested by hand and many people are needed to cultivate it. Machines have now been developed to do some of the work.

Rice producers of the world

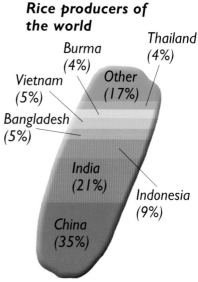

Thailand (4%)

Burma (4%)

Vietnam (5%)

Other (17%)

Bangladesh (5%)

India (21%)

Indonesia (9%)

China (35%)

RELIGIOUS BELIEFS

Colourful religions

India, the world's second most populous nation, has given the world two major religions – Buddhism and Hinduism. Today, Buddhists are found mainly in Thailand, Sri Lanka, Burma, Cambodia, China and Japan, rather than India where it began. In India the majority now follows Hinduism, which is probably the oldest major religion in the world. Asian countries, where Buddhism is a major religion, have adopted many customs of the West, particularly Japan and Thailand. Both Hindus and Buddhists have ornate temples.

Chinese New Year
Although China is in Northern Asia, many Chinese live in Southeast Asia. These communities celebrate Chinese New Year with festivals, including the 'dragon dance'.

Gods and goddesses

Hindus believe in a great god called Vishnu, a destroyer god (Shiva) and a goddess (Devi). These gods take many different forms and there are hundreds of minor gods. Temples are dedicated to particular gods.

Holy lives

Many Buddhists follow a monk's life, even if only for a time — it is perfectly normal for men to become monks for a short while. They wear yellow robes and carry food bowls with which they seek donations from the public.

Holy Cow

To Hindus, cows are held to be sacred and allowed to wander undisturbed, even in towns. India has more cattle than any other country. Although cows are milked, Hindus never kill cows to eat. One Indian in ten is vegetarian.

THE CLIMATE OF SOUTHERN ASIA

The rainy season

The countries in southern Asia are near enough to the tropics to be hot. Southeast Asia, near the Equator, has a climate like the tropical rainforest of Africa – hot and wet all year round. But India and Bangladesh, which are farther north, have more seasonal variation. In summer, when the Sun is overhead, central Asia gets very hot – it is too far inland for the sea to cool it down. Hot air rises over central Asia and, to take its place, cooler air is drawn in from over the Indian Ocean. This air has travelled a long way over the sea and so is very moist. When it reaches hills in India, Pakistan and Bangladesh, it is pushed up, and cools down to give huge quantities of rain. This wet season is called the monsoon.

Weather in Bombay, India

Average temperature:
25°C – December
29°C – June

Average rainfall:
508 mm – December
0 mm – June

Palm-fringed beaches
Large stretches of the coast of southern Asia are lined with dense vegetation that thrives in the tropical climate.

Wildlife

High temperatures and heavy rainfall encourage forests to grow. In the dry season, tropical grasses flourish. These habitats suit the Indian elephant.

Climate zones

Mountains

Temperate

Tropical rainforest

Desert

Evaporation due to Sun

Air forced to rise

Monsoon reaches land

Weather patterns

Monsoon winds blow over India from the south-west between April and October. Before this, the weather is very hot and dry. People long for the rains to come, to cool the air and help the rice crop to grow.

Wettest in the world

When the very wet air carried by monsoon winds reaches India and Bangladesh, it is forced to rise over hills (left). As it rises, the air cools, and deposits the moisture as rain. The wettest place in the world is Cherrapungi in north-east India, where once 26,461 mm of rain fell in one year.

ANCIENT MONUMENTS

Royal monuments

The ancient civilizations of the Near East left remarkable monuments behind. Among the most famous are the Great Pyramids in Egypt, which are around 4500 years old. Built by the pharaohs (kings) of Egypt as tombs, the pyramids are also thought to record the pattern of the stars in the sky. Next to the pyramids is the even older Sphinx, a stone lion with a human face. These ancient remains attract nearly 4 million tourists every year.

Legendary animal
The Giant Sphinx – 20 m in height – is the largest of thousands of sphinxes, many of which have wings and the head of a hawk.

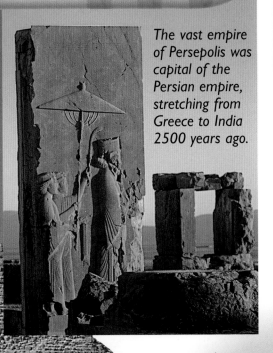

The vast empire of Persepolis was capital of the Persian empire, stretching from Greece to India 2500 years ago.

Off the map

Some of the historic sites in this region are not yet famous in the wider world. For various reasons, both religious and political, these places are off the tourist map. Iraq is isolated for political reasons, so no tourists visit the remains of ancient Babylon. Since the Islamic Revolution in Iran, few outsiders have visited the stunning ruins of Persepolis there.

Great Mosque, Mali

Many of the ancient buildings in Northern Africa were built as places of worship. The Great Mosque at Djenne, in Mali, is the largest mud–brick building in the world. Mud bricks do not last, so it has been rebuilt several times, most recently in 1905.

Istanbul

Built on either side of a narrow sea, Istanbul in Turkey is half in Europe, half in Asia. Founded by the Romans, Istanbul is famous for its palaces and mosques, as well as indoor markets, bazaars and grand architecture.

DESERT COUNTRIES

From oasis to big city

Much of North Africa and the Middle East is desert. Farming is limited to river valleys, such as the densely populated Nile Valley in Egypt where river water is used for irrigation. People also live in some hilly areas with better rainfall and oases – isolated fertile patches in the desert where water is found. Otherwise big cities are on the coast where trade and industries are most developed. Oil and natural gas have transformed countries such as Saudi Arabia, Libya and the UAE. These countries do not have enough people to fill all the new jobs. So, people come from overpopulated poorer neighbours, such as Yemen and Palestine, to work.

Ship of the Desert
Camels are called 'ships of the desert' because they are suited to life in the dry sands of Arabia, where they can travel 50 km a day. Camels can go for days without water and their wide feet do not sink in the sand.

Dubai

Sixty years ago, Dubai was little more than a fishing village. Now it is a booming modern city with great highways, an airport, a massive container port, factories, gleaming fashionable shops and luxury hotels. All this has happened because the state of Dubai is rich in oil.

Shopping

The shopping areas of the cities of North Africa and the Middle East used to be bazaars – narrow streets lined with tiny shops and stalls. In the large cities the bazaars now mainly sell souvenirs to visitors.

OIL

Striking oil

Oil has brought development and riches into desert regions where previously, there was little reason for anyone to choose to live there. The Gulf coast of Saudi Arabia and the United Arab Emirates (UAE) is now lined with oilfields, modern ports and cities. To help run the fields, and to provide all kinds of services in the fast-developing and wealthy cities such as Dubai, people have migrated from other parts of Asia and Europe – in the UAE over half the population comes from India and Pakistan.

Oil wars
Oil caused wars in the 20th century. In 1990 Iraq invaded its small oil-rich neighbour Kuwait. A US-led force freed Kuwait in 1991 but retreating Iraqis set fire to Kuwait's oil wells.

Riches of the Desert
The huge expanse of the Saudi desert is dotted with oil refineries.

Oil distribution

Oil is the basis of modern industry and transport. However, it is seldom found where it is needed. The major centres of the world's industry are in North America, western Europe and Japan – but the biggest oil-producing countries are in the Middle East.

Oil consumption

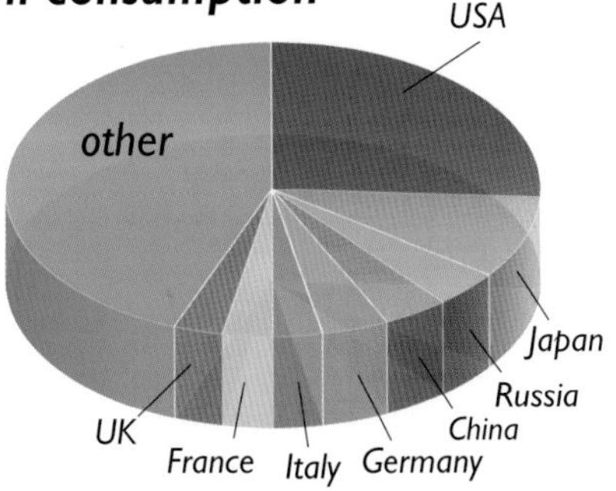

USA
other
Japan
Russia
China
Germany
Italy
France
UK

Oil production

Saudi Arabia
other
USA
Iran
Venezuela
Mexico
Norway
UAE

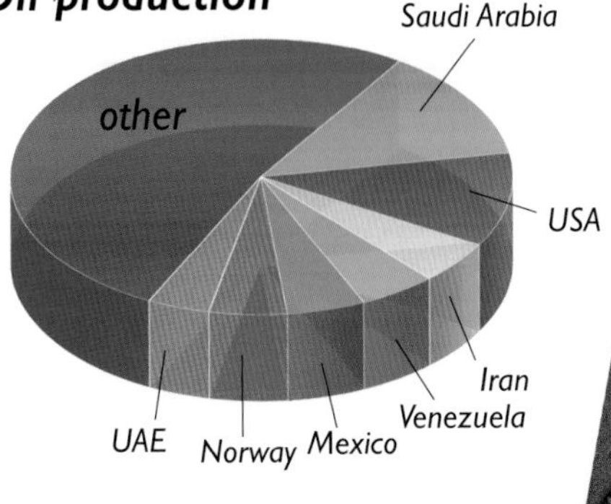

Wealth and poverty

The oil states of the Gulf (Saudi Arabia, the UAE and Kuwait) and Libya have grown rich on oil, but the Middle East and North Africa is a region of contrasts. Whereas the Gulf states have a high standard of living, poverty remains in countries with little or no oil, such as Yemen.

Daily prayers

The main influence on people's lives in this region is religion – Islam. Islam means submission – Muslims are people who submit themselves to Allah (God) by accepting Islam. Muslims pray five times a day. The call to prayer is broadcast from the minaret (tower) of a mosque. Attendance at a mosque is optional, but men usually go to the mosque on Friday.

Diet and dress

Customs and diet are influenced by climate and religion. Flat bread, fruit and vegetables are important parts of the diet, but people do not eat pork for religious reasons. Long, loose clothing is designed to keep cool, but Islam also says women must wear modest clothes.

Religious pilgrimage

All Muslims who can afford to are expected to make the pilgrimage to the holy cities in Saudi Arabia at least once. Each year millions of Muslims go on the pilgrimage (the hajj). They visit Mecca, the site of an ancient sacred rock (the Kaaba) and the city where the holy book of Islam, the Qu'ran, was revealed to the Prophet Muhammad. The hajj also involves visiting Medina, the city to which Muhammad fled in 622.

Wailing Wall
The Wailing Wall in Jerusalem is practically all that remains of the Temple of Solomon, built in Biblical times. Jews pray at the Wall.

Conflict

There is continuing violence in the Holy Land between Israel and the Palestinians. The area is home to both, but they cannot yet agree a compromise to divide the land between them and to live peacefully as neighbours.

Dome of the Rock
The mosque on the Dome of the Rock dominates Jerusalem, a holy city to three world religions – Christianity, Islam and Judaism. Its future is contested by Israel, which says that Jerusalem is its capital, and by the Palestinians, who want it to be theirs.

AFRICAN CROPS

Plantations

Many of the crops exported from Central and Southern Africa come from plantations very large farms, most originally owned by foreigners in the period when African countries were colonies of European countries. Foreign companies still own many plantations but more land is returning to African ownership. The Ivory Coast in West Africa is the largest producer of cacao in the world.

Cacao producers of the world

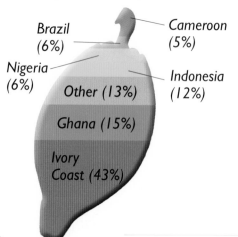

Brazil (6%)
Cameroon (5%)
Nigeria (6%)
Indonesia (12%)
Other (13%)
Ghana (15%)
Ivory Coast (43%)

Cash for crops
More African farmers grow crops to sell – cash crops – as well as food for themselves. These crops include coffee, cacao (which produces cocoa) and bananas.

Deforestation

Much forest has been cleared and a much bigger population means there are too many farmers wanting new land. In some African countries – such as Nigeria and Ghana – almost no forest is left. Only the Congo, Congo-Brazzaville, Cameroon and Gabon have large areas of forest still untouched by farming.

Hard work
Cassava, one of the main subsistence crops, is difficult to prepare. It is cleaned and crushed in a bowl by a club to get rid of all the poisonous liquid in it. From the flour, starchy porridge is made.

THE AFRICAN CLIMATE

A stable climate

Most of this region is near the Equator, so much of Africa is hot all year. As inland Africa is mainly flat plains, rather than high ranges of mountains that would form barriers against the movement of air, the climate is very similar over wide areas. In countries nearest to the Equator, the climate is much the same all year round – hot and wet. Mornings are clear, but by midday, clouds have started to form, and by late afternoon, thunderstorms begin and there is heavy rain.

Weather in the savannah

Bulawayo, Zimbabwe
Average temperature:
23°C – December
15°C – June

Average rainfall:
124 mm – December
2 mm – June

Weather in the rainforest

Gemena, Congo
Average temperature:
26°C – December
26°C – June

Average rainfall:
168 mm – December
155 mm – June

Open grassland

In the areas around the rainforest are the tropical grasslands called savannah. Trees and bushes are scarce and new grass grows only when the rainy season comes.

Steamy rainforests
High temperatures and heavy rainfall are ideal for the growth of trees in a broad band of rainforest running across central Africa. Trees in the forest grow up to 45 m in height. Their topmost branches form a canopy that almost blots out the sunlight.

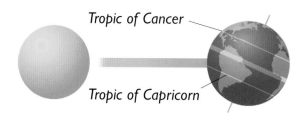

Tropic of Cancer

Tropic of Capricorn

Seasons
There is little seasonal variation in temperature near the Equator. Away from the Equator, there are seasons. The Sun is directly above the Equator in March and September, and above the Tropics of Cancer and Capricorn in June and December.

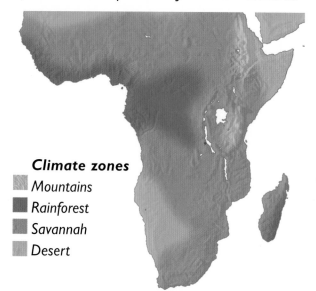

Climate zones
- Mountains
- Rainforest
- Savannah
- Desert

Lost forest
The forest is decreasing in size rapidly as it is felled for farming, destroying wildlife habitats and endangering plant species.

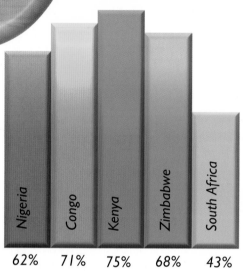

Nigeria	Congo	Kenya	Zimbabwe	South Africa
62%	71%	75%	68%	43%

Country dwellers

Most Africans are still farmers, herders and hunters. The percentage of people living in the country in typical African states is shown above.

Town and country

Town life and country life in modern Africa are very different. In most African countries the majority of people live in the country. Only South Africa, which has more big cities and industries than any other African country, is an exception.

Women pounding cassava ready to cook

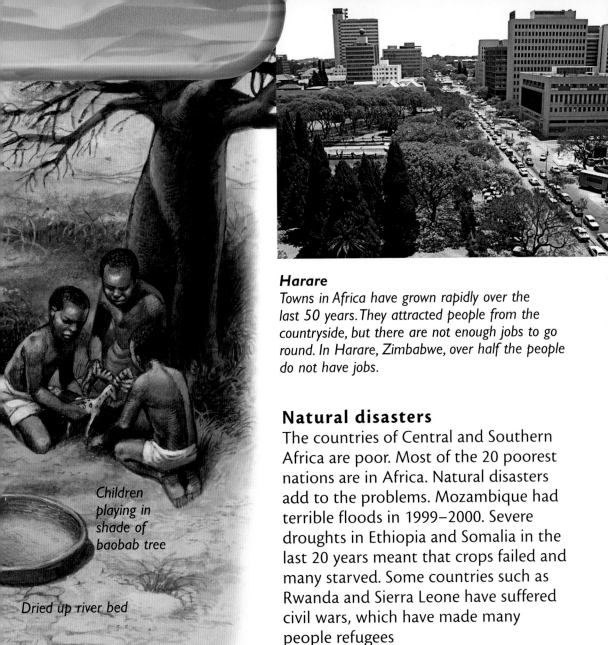

Harare

Towns in Africa have grown rapidly over the last 50 years. They attracted people from the countryside, but there are not enough jobs to go round. In Harare, Zimbabwe, over half the people do not have jobs.

Natural disasters

The countries of Central and Southern Africa are poor. Most of the 20 poorest nations are in Africa. Natural disasters add to the problems. Mozambique had terrible floods in 1999–2000. Severe droughts in Ethiopia and Somalia in the last 20 years meant that crops failed and many starved. Some countries such as Rwanda and Sierra Leone have suffered civil wars, which have made many people refugees

Children playing in shade of baobab tree

Dried up river bed

DESERT AND SAVANNAH

Plains and deserts

Less than one-third of Africa is forested – the rest is covered by either desert or tropical grassland called savannah. The Sahara, in the north, is the largest desert in the world. The Sahara is spreading south into Central Africa, partly because the climate is changing, and partly because people have damaged the land by trying to farm in dry areas next to the desert. Savannah regions are great plains of tall grasses with isolated clumps of trees. These grasslands vary from very dry to wet and lush with the seasons.

Savannah wildlife
The savannah grasslands of Africa are home to giraffes and vast herds of zebras, gazelles, antelopes and wildebeest, as well as lions and other big cats.

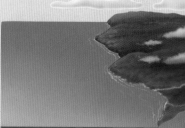

Moist air blows in from the sea

Water tank

The plants of the savannah are well adapted to life with one dry season and one wet season. The grasses die back in the dry season and spring up again when the rains come. Trees such as the baobab (right) store water in their thick trunks to use during the drought.

'Rain shadow' affects desert formation

Deserts form when land does not receive moist winds from the sea. For example, in the Namib Desert in Southern Africa, a dry wind blows from the land out to the sea. Other deserts might lie beyond (in the shadow of) mountains, where the clouds rise over the peaks and deposit rainfall on one side of the mountain range, and are 'empty' when they reach the far side (below).

Rain falls

Warm, moist air rises

Dry air blows inland

PRIMAL RELIGIONS

Old and new

Oceania is dominated by Australia and New Zealand, two modern countries. The tiny island nations of the Pacific are adopting the customs of the West. Although the majority of people in Oceania are Christian, there are still ancient religions known as 'primal religions'. Primal means 'first' because these religions were there long before the major world religions arrived. People who follow primal religions usually believe in a supreme god, but also in many other lesser gods and spirits.

Maoris

In New Zealand, three people in every 20 are Maoris, the original inhabitants. Most Maoris are now town-dwellers and there are few traditional houses remaining.

Uluru

Uluru (once called Ayers Rock), is known as the 'red heart' of Australia. This massive rock, 350 m in height and over 3.5 km in length, is one of the most sacred sites of Australia's Aborigines. It changes colour according to the direction of the Sun.

Aboriginal artefacts

The Aborigines of Australia once had no fixed homes and wandered Australia hunting and gathering roots and fruit. The Aborigines drew colourful rock paintings and carved boomerangs and other objects.

Pacific worship

The Pacific islands have been largely Christian for 100 years. As each island or group of islands often received missionaries from just one Church, today many island groups belong mainly to one religion – Tonga, for example, is Methodist.

CHANGING SCENERY

Different types of land

The Pacific Ocean covers just over one third of the world. Stretched across this ocean is the world's smallest continent, Oceania, made up of thousands of islands. Some are the tops of mountains or volcanoes, others have been built by coral. In the vast Pacific, islands occupy less than one percent of the total area. Alongside these small islands are four larger ones – Australia, New Guinea and the North and South Islands of New Zealand. Between them, these four islands have a remarkable variety of scenery including high, jagged mountains, dense tropical jungles, barren icy hills, wide sandy deserts and fertile sub-tropical lowlands.

1. Opening in Earth's crust

Coral Atoll Islands

Many Oceanian islands are made of coral. These islands, in the form of long reefs and round atolls, develop when coral grows up in shallow tropical seas. The Great Barrier Reef, at 2027 km in length, is the largest living structure on Earth. The largest coral atoll, Kwajalein in the Marshall Islands, encloses a huge lagoon within its outer ring of 'land'.

2. Molten rock wells up

3. Volcano erupts

Volcano formation

Volcanoes are mountains built up above an opening in the Earth's crust. Through this opening, molten rock (magma) wells up and is often thrown out with great force. Most volcanoes occur along the edges of the world's tectonic plates and a ring of volcanoes lines the Pacific Ocean. Volcanoes can erupt under the sea (left) and sometimes surface in Oceania as new islands.

New Zealand

Where molten rock is close to the ground it can heat up underground water. This produces hot springs, which are common in volcanic regions such as the Rotorua region of the North Island of New Zealand. Some hot springs called geysers eject hot water and steam in sudden spectacular eruptions. There are also boiling mud pools. These volcanic features attract tourists and the natural hot water is used for heating houses.

COUNTRIES OF OCEANIA

Tiny new countries

Oceania is a region of young countries. Over the last 100 years, the island nations have been colonies of the US, Britain, France, Japan and Germany – and later, Australia and New Zealand, too. Since the 1960s, groups of islands such as Fiji have become independent. These small countries have few resources. Most rely upon economic help from the countries that used to rule them, but the islands now aim for greater independence by working closely with each other.

Youthful city

Australia is the 'oldest' country in Oceania, having been founded in 1901. Sydney, Australia's biggest city, is only 200 years old. The Sydney Opera House is one of the world's most distinctive buildings. The radical sail-like roofs were said to have been inspired by sea shells.

'Discovery' of Oceania

Our history books usually tell us about the discovery of the islands of Oceania by Spanish, Dutch and British navigators, such as Magellan and Cook. However, these islands had already been discovered, and settled, by Polynesians, Melanesians and Micronesians who originally came from Asia more than 2000 years ago. When Europeans reached Oceania 500 years ago, they found these peoples established as farmers and fishermen. The Micronesian Maoris reached New Zealand 1000 years before Europeans.

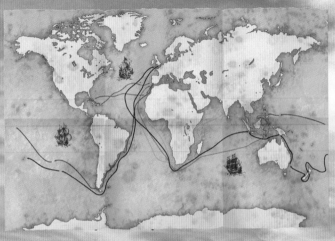

════════ 1492 Christopher Columbus
════════ 1497–98 Vasco Da Gama
════════ 1519–21 Magellan
▬ ▬ ▬ ▬ Completed by Del Cano 1522
════════ 1768–71 James Cook

Magellan

Working abroad

The small Pacific nations have rapidly increasing populations and there is not enough work for everyone. Large numbers of people are leaving the Oceanian islands to work in New Zealand, the USA and Australia. Some islands have more people living abroad than they do at home. The Cook Islands (above) have a population of 18,000 but there are another 21,000 Cook Islanders working in New Zealand.

POLLUTION

Threat to islands

The rise in industry, particularly in North America, northern Europe, China and Japan, has brought wealth but it has also created problems. Smoke from industrial chimneys releases harmful chemicals into the air. Car exhaust fumes add to the pollution. However, it is the greenhouse effect and global warming that are the biggest danger. Ice in the polar regions will melt and raise sea levels. By 2050, the sea will have risen by about 50 cm and the islands of Oceania will begin to suffer. A rise of one metre would drown nearly all of the nation of Tuvalu and most of its neighbour, Kiribati.

Reef damage

Coral reefs may look robust, but coral (right) is fragile. It is formed from the 'skeletons' of tiny creatures and is easily damaged by fishing. Polluted water and an increase in sea temperature, owing to global warming have killed billions of the tiny creatures that make coral. As a result, more than one-third of the world's coral reefs is now dead.

Islands lying low

Oceania consists of thousands of small low-lying islands made from coral. Many of these islands may disappear under the waves of the Pacific Ocean as the sea level rises because the planet is getting warmer. The islanders will have to find new homes, probably in the USA, New Zealand and Australia where many people have already moved from the more overcrowded islands.

carbon dioxide in atmosphere

Sun's rays

some heat is reflected back into space

heat trapped inside the atmosphere

heat penetrates atmosphere to reach Earth's surface

The greenhouse effect

Carbon dioxide is released into the atmosphere by burning coal and oil (fossil fuels). This gas threatens the environment by making the Earth's atmosphere warmer. This is known as the greenhouse effect (above) because carbon dioxide in the atmosphere acts like glass in a greenhouse. Just as glass traps heat inside, carbon dioxide traps heat in the atmosphere.

Polluted beaches

The small islands of Oceania have a problem disposing of waste and sewage and have sometimes resorted to dumping it at sea. The result has been unpleasant pollution of beaches and sea water, and also the death of fish and other marine life.

CLAIMING TERRITORY

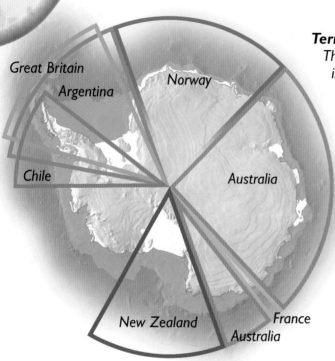

Great Britain
Argentina
Norway
Chile
Australia
New Zealand
France
Australia

Territorial claims

The map (left) shows the current international claims on Antarctica made by seven countries.

A dog's life

Roald Amundsen's team used lightweight dogsleds. If a dog died or became too weak to continue, it was fed to the other dogs. This reduced the amount of food that the men had to carry.

Disputed boundaries

Antarctica is home to bases established by 19 different countries. Various chunks of Antarctica are claimed by seven different countries – Britain, Australia, New Zealand, Norway, France, Chile and Argentina – and in places these claims overlap. Ownership of the land may one day become important because of possible mineral deposits.

Final frontier

Before the 20th century the polar regions – the areas around the North Pole and the frozen continent of Antarctica – were largely uninhabited and even unexplored. The polar regions are the world's 'last frontier'. The climate is harsh – in many areas the snow and ice never melt. There have been good reasons for people to brave the cold – to further research and search for new mineral sources.

Unexplored regions

There is much still to learn about what lies under the polar ice. There is also no precise map of the coastline of Antarctica. Gradually scientists are making astonishing discoveries – none greater than the recent discovery of a huge lake under the ice. Lake Vostok, in eastern Antarctica lies under 4000 m of ice.

Robert Scott

The British naval officer Robert Scott (right) commanded two Antarctic expeditions, but died on his return journey from the Pole in 1912. He had been beaten to the Pole by the Norwegian explorer Roald Amundsen. French and Russian explorers also played an important part in mapping Antarctica.

349

Mines

The polar wastes of Antarctica and the Arctic islands were some of the last areas on Earth to remain untouched by humans. Even here – and in the far north of Russia, North America and in Greenland – human activity is damaging nature. Scientists search for valuable minerals in these frozen places, as deposits begin to be used up elsewhere. The United States is now having difficulty supplying enough oil and natural gas for its needs. Large-scale development is taking place in northern Alaska to extract these fuels, even though the area is protected.

Midnight sun
Near the poles, the Sun is visible at midnight in summer. Tourists are attracted to view the 'midnight Sun'. Conservationists fear that the small, but growing, number of tourists to polar regions may damage an almost untouched environment.

Rocky coasts
There is evidence in polar regions to show that human activity is changing the Earth's climate. The planet is getting warmer, causing the ice in Antarctica, Greenland and around the North Pole to melt. Bare rock is already showing along some of the coasts of Antarctica, where before there was thick ice.

Protecting our environment

High up in the Earth's atmosphere, the ozone layer acts like a filter, protecting us from harmful radiation from the Sun. Gases that were once used in aerosol sprays and refrigerators (CFCs) and fire extinguishers (halons) were very damaging to this ozone. A hole in the ozone layer above Antarctica was first noticed in 1985, and continued to grow in size. Scientists realized what was causing this to happen and as a result, governments worldwide decided to ban the use of CFCs and halons.

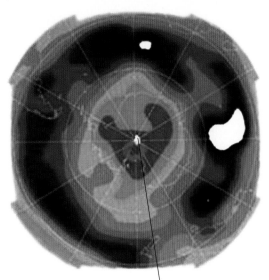

Ozone hole

Icebergs

In the last 25 years the ice sheets at the North and South Poles have been melting, due to global warming. Larger chunks of ice have been breaking away from the icecaps to form icebergs.

THE POLAR CLIMATE

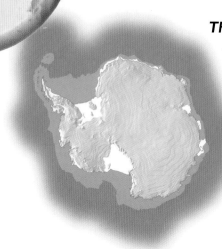

The coldest pole
Antarctica is generally colder than the Arctic because it is more mountainous. The coldest temperature ever recorded was at the Russian Antarctic scientific base Vostok in 1983, when the temperature fell to nearly -83°C.

Summer in the Arctic
In northern Russia and Canada is a snowy landscape called tundra. Ice in the soil melts during summer, making the land into a boggy marsh.

Changing lifestyle
The Inuits of northern Canada and Greenland once lived in igloos – small round houses made of ice blocks. Today, igloos are only made as temporary shelters. Many Inuits, particularly in Greenland, live in flats in towns.

Tropic of Cancer

Tropic of Capricorn

Cold extremes
The polar regions are too far from the Equator for the Sun ever to be overhead, or for there to be much seasonal difference in temperature.

Cold air descending

In polar regions, cold air from higher up in the atmosphere drops down to the Earth's surface. At surface level, this cold air flows away from the poles. There is no warm air blowing in from the south to ease the severity of the cold wind. The sea around Antarctica and the Arctic freezes over during winter, when it is coldest. In the past in Antarctica, the frozen ice appeared to almost double the size of the continent. As the planet warms up due to global warming, the amount of frozen sea around Antarctica is getting smaller.

Weather in Longyearbyen

Average temperature:
-15°C – December
2°C – June

Average rainfall/snow:
38 mm, snow – December
10 mm – June

Permanent camps

At any one time, there are scientific expeditions from more than 25 countries happening in the Arctic and Antarctica. Scientists may set up temporary camps, such as the one above, but permanent underground bases provide better protection against the cold.

Dry ice

The polar regions are called ice deserts. The air there is very dry. No moist air can be drawn in from the surrounding oceans to fill the space usually left by warm air rising. The little rain that does fall is frozen snow.

HIDDEN RESOURCES

Demand for minerals

Wherever there are minerals worth extracting, mining will occur. One day it might be worthwhile to extract natural wealth from under the icecaps of the North Pole and Antarctica – but not yet. It is not worthwhile mining in polar regions because it costs too much to recover minerals in such harsh conditions. However, when we run out of minerals elsewhere we will have to resort to mining polar regions.

Satellite survey
Hidden reserves of minerals can be found by surveying magnetically. A large deposit of iron is like a magnet. Surveying can be done from the air by plane or satellite.

Hidden resources
Occasionally ores – bodies of minerals – can be seen on the surface. In the polar regions, ores are hidden not only by layers of rock but under ice and snow.

Difficult conditions

If mining is ever to take place in Antarctica, a whole new type of mining industry will have to be invented. Working at such low temperatures, the ground will be frozen and difficult to dig. Exporting minerals by sea would be a problem when the sea is frozen around Antarctica for much of the year. Ships designed as icebreakers would need to be used, like the one shown below, as they have special hulls that can smash through the ice sheet.

Potential polar resources

Lead and zinc used to be mined in Greenland, but it is now too expensive to dig out what is left. Coal has been found under the frozen land of Svalbard, a group of Norwegian islands in the Arctic Circle. There is natural gas under Ellesmere Island and the Queen Elizabeth Islands far to the north of Canada. Zinc and lead deposits have also been found here, but they are not recovered yet.

Minerals in Antarctica

The large deposits of coal found in the Transantarctic Mountains would be too expensive to mine.

Evidence of iron ore has been found in the Transantarctic Mountains.

Gold has been found in small amounts in Queen Maud Land.

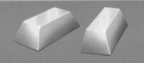

Copper has been traced in the Antarctic peninsula.

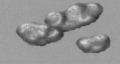

Natural Gas has been found in the Ross Sea.

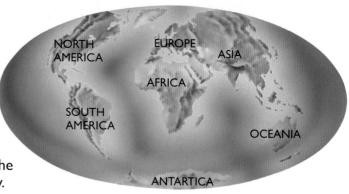

Super continent

Some 280 million years ago all the continents were joined in one huge landmass, called Pangaea. Over time, this 'super continent' broke up and the landmasses drifted apart to form the continents as we know them today.

NORTH AMERICA
EUROPE
ASIA
AFRICA
SOUTH AMERICA
OCEANIA
ANTARTICA

Terrifying twisters

A tornado is a windstorm that creates a huge funnel of whirling air stretching down to the ground. The tip of the funnel sucks up everything in its track. In the United States tornadoes are called 'twisters'. They roar across the Midwest at speeds of 50 km/h.

Driest desert

The driest place on Earth is the Atacama Desert in Chile, South America. Intervals between showers may be as long as 100 years, and in some areas it has not rained for more than 400 years.

Huge hailstones

The biggest hailstone fell in Coffeyville, Kansas, USA, in 1970. It was 44.5 cm in diameter, and weighed nearly one kilogram – bigger and heavier than a tennis ball.

Ancient rocks

The rocks at the bottom of the Grand Canyon are 2 billion years old. The Colorado River in the United States has worn away tonnes of rock, creating a huge canyon that extends 446 km. In places, the canyon is 1.6 km deep and 29 km wide.

Volcanic explosions

Kilauea, a volcano in Hawaii, is the world's biggest active volcano. Since its most recent outburst in 1983, it has been spouting fountains of fire and a river of red-hot lava.

AMAZING FACTS AND FIGURES

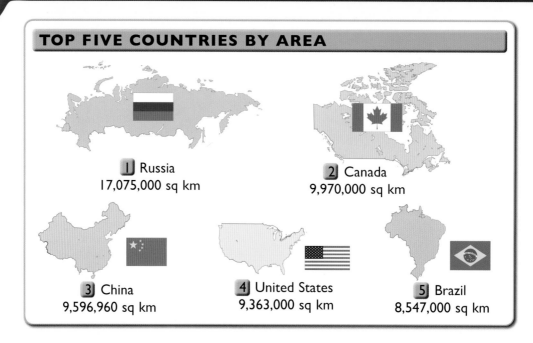

TOP FIVE COUNTRIES BY AREA

1 Russia
17,075,000 sq km

2 Canada
9,970,000 sq km

3 China
9,596,960 sq km

4 United States
9,363,000 sq km

5 Brazil
8,547,000 sq km

HIGHEST FALLS

Falls	Country	Drop
1 Angel	Venezuela	979 m
2 Tugela	Africa	947 m
3 Utigård	Norway	800 m
4 Mongefossen	Norway	774 m
5 Yosemite	USA	739 m
6 Østre Mardøla Foss	Norway	656 m

Angel Falls

Mount Everest

THE HIGHEST PEAKS

1	Everest	8848 m
2	K2	8610 m
3	Kanchenjunga	8598 m
4	Lhotse	8511 m
5	Makalu	8481 m

Note: All these mountains are in the Himalayas

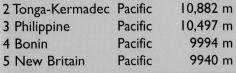

DEEPEST OCEAN TRENCHES

Trench	Ocean	Depth
1 Marianas	Pacific	10,911 m
2 Tonga-Kermadec	Pacific	10,882 m
3 Philippine	Pacific	10,497 m
4 Bonin	Pacific	9994 m
5 New Britain	Pacific	9940 m

Marianas Trench

GLOSSARY

Aestivation
The period of animal inactivity during the summer.

Afterlife
A belief held by the ancient Egyptians that life continued after death.

Agriculture
The process of cultivating the land, such as growing crops.

Alloy
A mixture of two or more metals, or a metal and a non-metal.

Amphibian
An animal that lives partly on land and partly in water.

Apartheid
The South African policy of keeping different races of people apart (1949–1990).

Aquatic
Living in water.

Artillery
Heavy long-range guns.

Atmosphere
The layer of air that surrounds the Earth. It is 700 km deep.

Atom
The smallest part of an element.

Camouflage
A disguise produced by colour, pattern or shape, which makes an animal difficult to see.

Carnivore
An animal that mainly eats meat.

Catalyst
A substance that improves the rate of a chemical reaction, remaining unchanged itself.

Cavalry
The part of an army that is made up of soldiers on horseback.

Civil war
A war fought between groups of people from and in the same country or region.

Climate
The term given to types of weather over a period of time.

Colony
An area of land ruled by another country.

Combustion
A chemical reaction in which a substance combines with oxygen and gives off heat and light.

Communism
A form of government where the state owns all the land and provides for people's needs.

Conduction
The process that allows heat to be transferred from one part of a substance to another.

Convection
The movement of molecules from a warmer place to a cooler place, such as in liquid or gas.

Depression
A period of severe decline in economic activity, causing unemployment and hardship.

Democracy
A form of government based on the rule of the people, usually through elected representatives.

Dictator
A ruler with absolute power, usually unelected and ruling by force.

Drought
A long period of dry weather without rain.

Electrolysis
The passing of electricity through a liquid that contains ions in order to produce a chemical reaction.

Empire
A state and the conquered lands it rules over.

Equator
An imaginary line around the Earth, equal in distance between the North and South Poles.

Erosion
The process of wearing away the Earth's surface – mainly caused by water, wind and ice.

Expansion
The process by which a substance, remaining the same in mass, increases in volume.

Export
The sale of goods to another country.

Famine
A shortage of food often causing people to die of starvation.

Fault
A break or line of weakness in the Earth's crust.

Force
The push or pull that makes something move, slows it down or stops it, or the pressure that something exerts on an object.

Friction
A force that is created when a solid object rubs against another or when it moves through a liquid or gas.

Gravity
The force that pulls objects towards the ground.

Global warming
The increase in the Earth's temperature caused by too much carbon dioxide in the atmosphere.

Habitat
The particular area or natural place where a group of plants or animals live, such as deserts, lakes and grassland.

Herbivore
An animal that only eats plants.

Hibernation
When animals go to sleep for the winter. The animal lives off its stored fat reserves until the spring.

GLOSSARY

Incubate
To brood eggs in order to hatch young.

Infantry
The foot-soldiers of an army.

Ion
An atom that has lost or gained electrons and carries an electrical charge.

Irrigation
The watering of the land by artificial methods, usually to help the growth of food crops.

Larva
The grub of an insect.

Life cycle
The stages through which a creature passes from fertilization to death.

Magnetic field
An area around the poles of a magnet in which the magnet can exert a force.

Marsupial
A mammal that gives birth to tiny young that finish developing in a pouch.

Mass
The amount of material an object contains. An object's mass never changes. Its weight depends on gravity.

Migration
The regular journey by certain animals to a place in order to breed or find better food supplies.

Molecule
The smallest amount of a chemical substance, made up of two or more atoms.

Myth
An ancient traditional story of gods and heroes.

Nuclear
Relating to or powered by the fission or fusion of atomic nuclei.

Parasite
A plant or animal that depends completely on another plant or animal in order to stay alive.

Parliament
An assembly of the representatives (usually elected) of a group or nation.

Plankton
Tiny animals that live in salt or fresh water.

Plantation
An area of land used to grow plants, such as cotton and tea, to be harvested and sold.

Plasma
An electrically charged gas made up of equal numbers of positive ions and free electrons.

Plate
The Earth's crust is divided into about 15 huge pieces called plates.

Photosynthesis
The process by which green plants make food from carbon dioxide and water.

Pollution
Damage to the environment caused by human activity.

Predator
An animal that feeds by hunting and killing other creatures.

Pressure
The force applied to a certain area.

Protestantism
A branch of the Christian Church that was started by Martin Luther in the 1500s.

Radioactivity
The emission of radiation from unstable elements by the splitting of their atomic nuclei.

Refugee
A person who flees to another country for shelter or protection.

Reptile
A cold-blooded scaly animal that lays eggs on land. Only a few give birth to live young.

Republic
A state without a king or queen, where the people elect their leader.

Reservoir
A man-made lake or tank used to store water.

Sanitation
Measures for the promotion of health and prevention of disease, particularly drainage and sewage disposal.

Satellite
A small body that orbits round a larger one. Earth has one satellite – the Moon. There are also many artificial satellites orbiting the Earth.

Scavenger
An animal that feeds on the flesh of dead animals (carrion).

Shanty town
An area where housing is makeshift.

Treaty
An agreement between two or more parties.

Tundra
The Arctic region of treeless land – the soil is frozen apart from the surface layer, which melts in the summer.

Vacuum
A region in which there is no matter.

Vegetation
The collective term for vegetable growth including plants, trees and flowers.

INDEX

INDEX

INDEX

S

INDEX